PEOPLE AT ODDS

NATIVE AMERICANS AND THE UNITED STATES

PEOPLE AT ODDS

THE BALKANS: PEOPLE IN CONFLICT

ENGLAND AND INDIA

INDIA AND PAKISTAN

THE IRA AND ENGLAND

ISRAEL AND THE ARAB WORLD

NATIVE AMERICANS AND THE UNITED STATES

PEOPLE AT ODDS

NATIVE AMERICANS AND THE UNITED STATES

Alison Turnbull Kelley

Chelsea House Publishers
Philadelphia

CHELSEA HOUSE PUBLISHERS

EDITOR IN CHIEF Sally Cheney
DIRECTOR OF PRODUCTION Kim Shinners
CREATIVE MANAGER Takeshi Takahashi
MANUFACTURING MANAGER Diann Grasse

Staff for **NATIVE AMERICANS AND THE UNITED STATES**

ASSISTANT EDITOR Susan Naab
PICTURE RESEARCHER Jaimie Winkler
PRODUCTION ASSISTANT Jaimie Winkler
COVER AND SERIES DESIGNER Keith Trego
LAYOUT 21st Century Publishing and Communications, Inc.

http://www.chelseahouse.com

First Printing

1 3 5 7 9 8 6 4 2

Library of Congress Cataloging-in-Publication Data

Kelley, Alison.
   Native Americans and the United States / by Alison Kelley.
      p. cm. — (People at odds)
Summary: Describes the years of conflict between Native Americans
and European settlers, and briefly mentions some attempts by the
United States government to make amends for some of the injustices
the Indians have suffered.
Includes bibliographical references and index.
   ISBN 0-7910-6707-6
   1. Indians of North America—Government relations—Juvenile literature.
2. Indians, Treatment of—United States—Juvenile literature. 3. Indians
of North America—Social conditions—Juvenile literature. [1. Indians
of North America—Government relations. 2. Indians, Treatment of.
3. Indians of North America—Social conditions.] I. Title. II. Series.
E93 .K286 2002
973.04'97—dc21

2001008107

CONTENTS

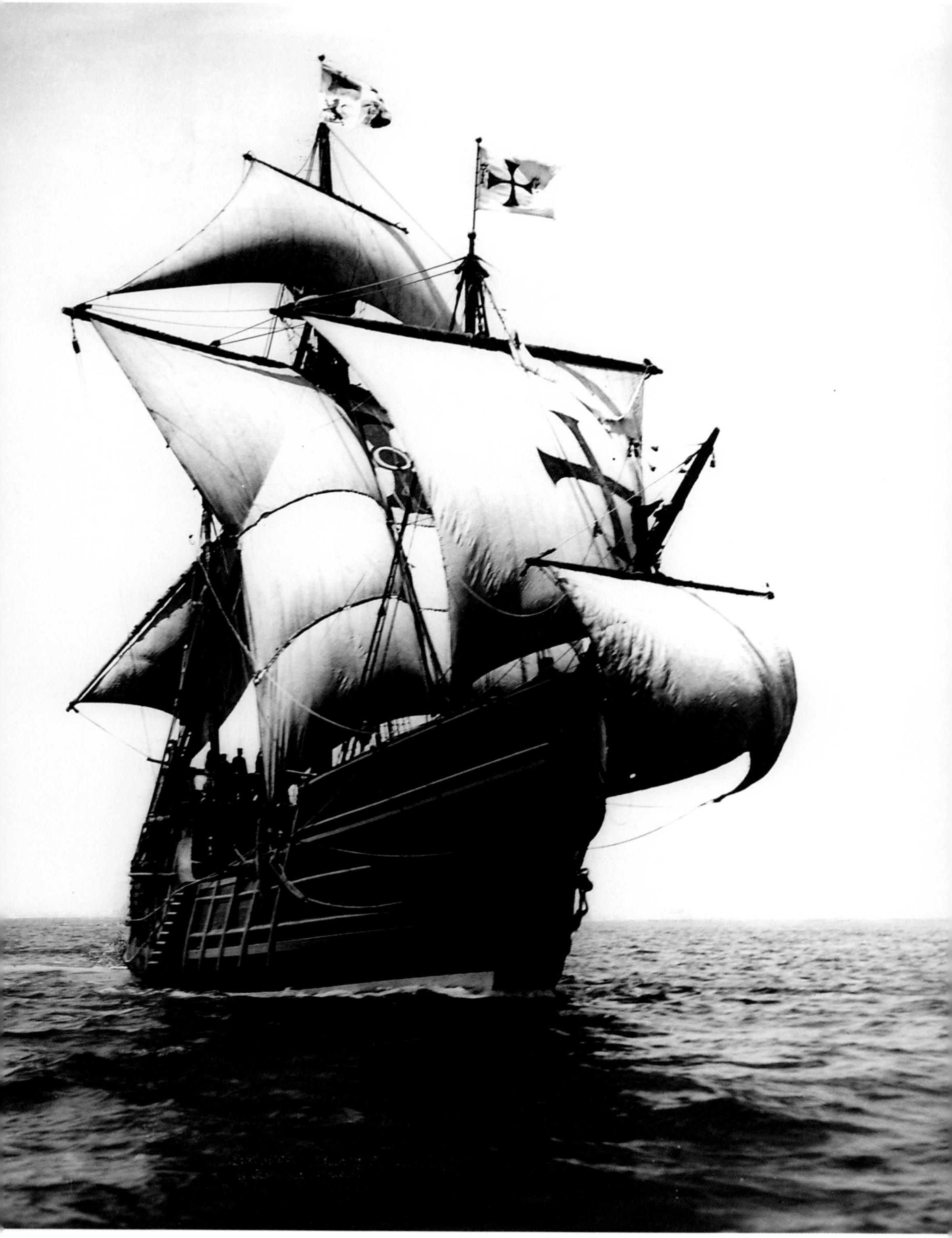

The First Americans

Macú (big eyes) and Maguamo (big trumpet [loud voice]) crouch behind a stand of palm trees. They watch intently as three strange-shaped objects slowly move toward shore. What are these strange things? What power moves them? The objects get closer, and the young braves move out of their hiding place to get a better look. The great sailing objects are ships. Standing on deck are men wearing brightly colored coverings on their bodies. How strange, the braves think, to cover the body! The mariners come ashore and soon see the boys watching them. They extend their arms in greeting. The two braves move forward and also make a sign of friendship. Then they run to tell the tribal elders.

Little did these Taino braves know that their lives were about to change forever. Thus began the Modern Age, and the world would never again be the same.

Christopher Columbus' ship sailed to North America in 1492. When he met the Native Americans he called them "Indians" because he believed he was in the West Indies.

An 1879 cartoon from *Harper's Weekly* emphasizes the brutality of the U.S. government policy dealing with the Native Americans.

◆　　◆　　◆

Christopher Columbus first landed with his small flotilla of ships, the *Nina*, *Pinta*, and *Santa Maria*, on an island in the Caribbean Sea, which came to be known as San Salvador. Even though history books credit Columbus with "discovering" America, neither he, nor the Spanish Conquistadors, nor even the first pilgrims who arrived at Plymouth Rock in 1620 are truly the first Americans.

Before the white man came, many natives inhabited the islands of the West Indies, as well as the continent of North America. These natives, whom we now call Native Americans, are the "First Americans," because for thousands of years they were the only human beings in the land now called the United States. How did they get here? The distant ancestors of these natives from the last Ice Age migrated to a "new world" many thousands of years ago.

MIGRANTS FROM AN ICE AGE

During the last Ice Age 30,000 to 50,000 years ago, groups of humans came long distances to North America from many parts of Asia. They traveled across a land bridge called *Beringia,* which joined Siberia and Alaska across the Bering Sea. Beringia joined the two continents of Asia and North America. The migrants were Japanese, Chinese, Tibetans, Burmese, Siamese, Malays, Lapps, Finns, Magyars, Turks, and many others. Migrating southward, they came to this new world not as adventurers or explorers, but as hunters following aimless herds of large animals. The animals they found were huge and plentiful: woolly mammoths, mastodons—both ancestors of the elephant—short-faced bears (larger than grizzlies), giant bison (ancestors of American buffalo), large armadillos, giant beavers, four-horned antelopes, and giant sloths. Smaller game were also plentiful, such as elk, deer, and camels.

For many years, the migrants traveled back and forth from Asia to different parts of Alaska searching for new sources of fish and large animals. For some thousands of years, they continued moving through Alaska across North America, ever in search of food resources. Over time, these migrants would build shelters with materials they found in this resource-rich new land. Archeological findings during the 1920s and 1930s showed that America was well populated during the end of the last Ice Age (the Paleo-Indian Period, about 13,000 B.C. to 7,900 B.C.).

GLACIERS AND MIGRATION

During the years of migration when the migrants were coming to North America, there were many gradual earth and weather changes. One force of nature in particular temporarily prevented the migrants from proceeding farther south across North America, and also prevented their return to their homelands in Asia. This force was the *glacier.*

Glaciers are large masses of ice that move slowly across land from slopes or mountainous areas. They either spread out over land or move toward a large body of water. Because glaciers are very deep and lock in and compress so much water, the sea level during the Paleo-Indian Period was about 400 feet lower than it is today. Modern coastal city areas such as New York were much farther inland than they are today. Gradually, new lakes formed where moving glaciers had gouged depressions in the earth. For example, many years ago almost the whole state of Nevada—now arid land—was a lake.

The slow and unpredictable movement of glaciers crossing the land at times caused the migrants to become land-locked in Alaska for centuries. Then, as changes in climate would cause the glaciers to recede, the land provided a path for the travelers to advance. Then the land bridge disappeared and reappeared as the glaciers partially melted and then refroze. Finally, warming weather conditions caused a vast melt, and

When peoples from the Asian continent crossed the land bridge thousands of years ago, huge glaciers covered most of North America. The large sheets of ice slowly rolled over the continent, carving out the landscape.

the large strip of land that bridged the two continents became submerged under water. Thus, the huge expansive land masses became separate and formed the two continents of Asia and North America.

MIGRATION CONTINUES

During the Paleo-Indian period of history, ice covered much of the land. The climate was colder and rainier in this glacial age than our climate today, and lakes and swampy areas were abundant. The people who lived far north in the tundra areas—what is now called Alaska— were fishermen and hunters. Over time, these early immigrants traveled farther into North America to the West and Northwest, to the Central Plains, and to the Atlantic forests in the East. They continued through Mexico and the jungles of Central America even to South America, all the while adapting to their environment. They found a land fertile with life-giving plants and animals. When animals periodically became scarce, plants sustained them.

The people who migrated to lands teeming with animals —especially large animals—were hunters. Those who migrated to coastal areas became fisherman. Those who later traveled to areas where the soil was fertile and lakes, rivers, and streams were abundant became farmers as well as fishermen. Still others became gatherers and foragers, searching for berries, nuts, edible plants, and roots. Each geographical area in the New World offered different challenges and different resources. Where animals were scarce and water was minimal and provided no fish, many traded goods with other tribes or families. Family groups learned how to live and survive according to the climate of the land where they lived and the land's natural resources.

These immigrants to the New World did not represent a single family group or even a single people. They came from many different parts of Asia, some of which were very distant from each other. Because of this, their way of life differed one from the other, and 200 or more languages and dialects were represented. Some of these first Americans came with a strict hierarchy of power and authority and wealth—sometimes according to their lineage. Others had no center of power at all. Even in prehistoric, times North America was a melting pot of cultures and ways of life.

ARCHAIC AND WOODLAND PERIODS

By around 8000 B.C., the climate of North America had changed. Ice began to melt. Deserts emerged, lakes went dry, and many large animals that thrived in the glacial age didn't adapt to the warmer climate. These great beasts gradually disappeared. This period, known as the *Archaic* (or *Foraging*) *Period*, lasted until about 1500 B.C. Day-to-day life changed for the first Americans. They no longer depended on "family foraging," in which family or tribal groups traveled across the land hunting for good food sources. Many began to raise their own crops.

In the West, the natives hunted waterfowl and rabbits and an occasional antelope. But they were mainly foragers, gathering roots, nuts, seeds, and fruit.

The eastern part of North America provided an abundance of edible plants, game, fish, and turtles. Small game—beavers, rabbits, opossums, turkeys, and squirrels—and larger game such as deer were also plentiful. By 3000 B.C., the natives had started farming. This practice had moved north from the Mexican highlands to the rest of North America. Early native peoples learned to cultivate the all-important maize, as well as pumpkins, amaranth (actually, the nutritious seed of the amaranth plant), and beans. Raising their own crops enabled the natives to stay together in towns rather than roam across the country in search of food. They established farming communities and even grew surpluses of food to set aside for winter sustenance. These farming communities progressed to become permanent villages.

Many tribes gathered food from the land as they hunted wandering herds. They also learned to cultivate food from the earth, including maize, pumpkins, and beans.

By 500 B.C., the *Woodland Period* had fully supplanted the Archaic Period. People of this era created and developed a culture that distinguishes them to this day. They made pottery and jewelry and built huge burial and ceremonial mounds. They continued farming maize and other crops.

HUNTERS

During the Paleo-Indian Period, what emerged was a succession of great tribal hunters.

The *Clovis* people (named from archeological findings at Clovis, New Mexico) developed Clovis points as weapons to fell large animals. These points were stones of about four to five inches long, which the natives had chipped and made very sharp. They attached these points to a wooden shaft and formed a spear. The sharpness of the points together with the great strength of the thrower made a formidable foe against even a large animal, such as the long-haired bison and the woolly mammoth. However, hunting such large animals required the cooperation of groups of hunters. And so they joined together in bands to corner small herds or force them over cliffs.

Later, the *Folsom* people and then the *Plano* people roamed the American Plains. The Planos hunted the giant bison, often driving an entire herd into a dangerous place such as an arroyo (gully), where they couldn't escape. Generally, the natives in the Plains specialized in large game, while their contemporaries in the Pacific Northwest focused on small mammals, camels, sloth, and fish. Unfortunately, hunters of large game who couldn't adapt to another way of survival, such as the Clovis and the Folsom peoples, eventually died out.

Over thousands of years, the very large animals disappeared. No more giant bison, large armadillos, and other giant animals roamed North America. They had become extinct. Historians aren't sure how this happened. Some scholars believe the native hunters depleted the herds with their hunting skills perfected over thousands of years. Others believe the warmer climate was the culprit, with less moisture and disappearing rivers and lakes. Climatic changes, too, may have affected the animals' breeding cycles. Maybe all of these reasons explain the extinction of the giant animals. Just as we'll never see a woolly mammoth or a mastodon, we'll never really know why the great beasts disappeared.

FORAGERS AND FARMERS

Prehistoric eras overlapped, depending on the geographic area. The *Desert Culture* is an example of a people whose skills and culture overlapped the Paleo-Indian Period through the Archaic Period. They were thriving at around the same time that the Plano and Folsom peoples were successfully hunting game. The difference is that the desert people were foraging during the Paleo-Indian Period, whereas most other cultures were mainly hunting. The desert people lived in the West—in what are now Nevada, California, Utah, and parts of Wyoming, Idaho, and Oregon. They focused on plants—collecting seeds and roots and using plant fibers to make baskets for carrying grains. They used *manos* and *metates,* stones that were like a primitive mortar and pestle for grinding grains.

The desert people became skilled in working with skins and hides. They made moccasins and body coverings. They made flour from nuts, mixed them with water, and cooked them. They were probably the first to cook food. The desert people also developed the skills of basket weaving and pottery making, which they refined and continued into modern times.

The *Adena-Hopewell Culture* (*Mound Builders*) of the Woodland Period (starting around 1000 B.C.) stood out not only for mound building but also for pottery making. They lived mainly in the Ohio Valley in small villages. The Adena-Hopewell and other Mound Builders had a strong belief in honoring their dead. They started by building low mounds over burial pits. Centuries later their mound building progressed to such an extent that numerous workers and many long hours were needed to erect gigantic serpentine mounds. Some mounds had many layers containing bodies. Special objects such as clay pipes, copper jewelry, and headdresses were buried with the dead. The Adena-Hopewell people were hunters, gatherers, and farmers. In addition to their building and craft skills, they were talented traders, who established links with tribes far and wide.

The *Mississippian Culture* of the southeast, also Mound Builders, didn't disappear until about 1750 A.D. The complexity and refinement of the mound structures and crafts of the Mississippians (as well as the Adena-Hopewell) indicate that they must have had a class structure to divide the labor for some of their monumental projects.

ARTIFACTS

As the great survivors traveled farther and farther across North America, they learned to adapt to the different climates and resources that the land offered. They made shelter, clothing, tools, and weapons. Some of these objects have been found. Objects found in North America that have endured hundreds and thousands of years prove that human beings inhabited North America—long before Christopher Columbus's ships ever arrived on San Salvador in the Caribbean and before the pilgrims led a steady stream of settlers from Europe. In what is now New Mexico, archeologists have unearthed ancient tools and weapons such as Clovis fluted points for hunting, dating back to 9000 B.C.

Petroglyphs can be seen today in New Mexico and Arizona. They are pictures carved and drawn into rocks by early natives hundreds to thousands of years ago. The Hopi Pueblo at Oraibi in northern Arizona was made almost 1,000 years ago. Other traces of early humans such as stone tools are still being found.

SOME BASIC DIFFERENCES BETWEEN EARLY NATIVE AMERICANS AND THE WHITE MAN

Language

The Native American and the white man showed great differences in language expression. The languages of early natives were unwritten. Their folktales and sacred stories embodied their history, culture, and literature. The first Americans took great pride in the telling and retelling of these stories. In fact, story-telling and speaking ability were admired as much as feats of bravery or accomplishments in battle.

Because Native Americans didn't rely on written words, they could not understand the value the white man placed on written language. The white man wanted everything of importance to be put into writing to give it permanency. Native Americans remembered spoken promises, but written words confused them. This lack of familiarity with written words made it easy to cheat the Indians, which was later done in treaties.

Many of the Native American languages have been translated into written form. Centuries ago, Christian missionaries helped the Native Americans to create an alphabet and a written language. Before the white man

Native Americans had no alphabetic written language like the Europeans. They passed down stories by telling them to others and used art to "write" a story.

arrived, there were more than 200 Native American languages and dialects. Today about 150 languages are still spoken—all quite different from each other, just like the tribes who speak them.

The English language has adopted many words from Native Americans. Examples are moose, raccoon, manatee, skunk, puma, maize, avocado, and blizzard. The names of many present-day American cities are borrowed from Indian names, such as Chicago, Seattle, Tallahassee, and Tucson. In states such as New Mexico, Native American influence is very strong and very visible.

Art

A contrast also existed between the Native American's and the white man's approach to art. The white man creates art for art's sake. Native American languages have no word for art. They created objects for their beauty *and* for their usefulness. Beautifully and colorfully woven blankets, colorfully decorated pottery, and well-made woven clothing are examples of how the Native American combines art with usefulness.

Religion and Spirituality

Native Americans have great respect for the earth and give thanks for all that it provides. Navajos call the land "Earth, My Mother." They believe that the earth is sacred and beautiful and doesn't need to improve. They believe that the Creator is the power behind the seasons. Ancient men believed that man belongs to nature and thus must live in harmony with it. They organized their lives around nature's cycles, especially the seasons. The Native American vision of nature is in the present. They appreciate the beauty of the trees in the forest and see all elements of nature as a "community living in the present moment." They usually offered a prayer of thanks and reparation when they hunted and killed an animal.

The white man views the earth in terms of progress and what the land will do for them. They don't view themselves as a part of nature, but rather as something separate from it. With their focus on progress, the white man saw the Native Americans' way of life as inferior to their own, and felt they had a right to change Native Americans to civilize them. In their misguided attempt at civilizing the native peoples, the white man took their land and thereby destroyed their culture. These deep differences in how the white man and the Native American think about nature and the steward-ship of the land sowed the seeds of many conflicts.

Even though all native populations had great diversity in language and customs, their religious beliefs were based mainly on nature mysticism and oriented toward a supreme being. Much ritual was built into their belief systems. They believed that all things have a soul or spirit. This explains their great respect for the earth and for all beings, even the animals that they hunt. The Native Americans' strong religious and spiritual beliefs have survived until today. We believe that their beliefs related to nature and a supreme creator go back for thousands of years. Their spirituality was handed down and derived from the beliefs of long-ago ancestors.

Such was the society of the First Americans—a spiritual, structured, and skillful people, neither barbaric nor infantile —into which the first Europeans arrived.

The Arrival of the White Man

CHRISTOPHER COLUMBUS

Standing on the prow of the Santa Maria, *Christopher Columbus is bursting with pride thinking about carrying Spain's royal banners ashore. He is exhausted from the long voyage, but happy because he will claim this land for Spain.*

In 1492, Christopher Columbus set sail from Spain to find a new trade route to the Far East and India and to bring honor to Queen Isabella for Spain. He thought he had reached the East Indies (the Far East). But his small flotilla of three ships had really landed on an island in the West Indies, now called San Salvador. Columbus' voyage was a turning point in time because it opened the gates for all of Europe to discover a New World.

Columbus later sailed to other islands of the West Indies—islands now called St. Croix, Haiti, Puerto Rico, and finally Cuba—claiming them for Spain by setting down the Spanish flag. Later expeditions brought Columbus to Central America

Native Americans watch Christopher Columbus' ships approaching. When Columbus landed, the natives' willingness to share surprised him.

and South America. Ironically, Christopher Columbus never landed on the continent of North America, although he is credited with "discovering" America.

When Columbus saw the darker skin color of the island inhabitants, he called them *los Indios* (Indians, people from India). The Arawak-speaking Taino natives thought Columbus and his men came from heaven, and so they were very friendly and even in awe of the visitors. They didn't know how much their lives would change—and not for the better.

Columbus probably did not have cruel intentions, but clearly he didn't value the friendly native inhabitants whom he met on his voyages. He wrote:

> The people of this island, and all the other islands which I have found and of which I have information, all go naked, men and women, as their mothers bore them. . . . They have no iron or steel or weapons, nor are they fitted to use them, not because they are not well-built men and of handsome stature, but because they are marvelously timorous. . . .they never refuse anything which they possess, if it be asked of them; on the contrary, they invite anyone to share it, and display as much love as they would give their hearts, and whether the thing be of value or whether it be of small price, at once with whatever trifle of whatever kind it may be that is given to them, with that they are content.

He described them as . . . "A loving people without covetousness. . . . Their speech is the sweetest and the gentlest in the world."

Columbus and the seafaring Spaniards seemed to make friends with the natives, but they actually took advantage of them. Columbus took some natives from each island back to Spain to use as slaves and to prove to Queen Isabella that they lived on the land he discovered. Columbus said: "And as soon as I arrived in the Indies, in the first island, which I found, I took by force some of them." Unfortunately, only seven natives survived the first voyage back to Spain.

Columbus wrote to his superiors in Spain, describing the abundance of gold, spices, cotton, aloe wood, and slaves, "as many as they shall order to be shipped and who will be from the idolators." News of the New World spread throughout Europe. Hearing of such riches, many greedy and vicious Spanish explorers set out to conquer this New World.

SPANISH INVADERS

The Spaniards began their conquest in 1513, with Ponce de Léon. Thereafter, a succession of Spanish invaders called conquistadors ("conquerors") came to the West Indies and to North America. Like Columbus, they captured Taino natives from the islands. They made them work as slaves on plantations and in mines. Bahama Indians were sold as slaves for 4 peços (Spanish currency) each. Life was changing quickly for the natives of the West Indies.

Coming up from the Florida coast, the Spanish Conquistadors burned, destroyed, killed, and made slaves of the natives they encountered. They had a lust for gold as a symbol of power and a determination for proselytizing (preaching to convert to a religion) and converting the native peoples. Spanish nonclerics were religious fanatics and interpreted conversion not in a spiritual or religious manner. In other words, they desired to make the Indians submit to Spanish beliefs and thus be under their dominion. Their underlying motive was to gain gold and riches.

The Spaniards were a highly purposeful people; the Indians were accustomed to living in the moment. No wonder that the Indians did not understand this kind of thinking. Also, the early white settlers in general, especially Jesuit priests, misinterpreted the rituals and ceremonies of the Native American as pagan forms of worship. This was cause for a great and continuing misunderstanding between the two cultures.

In the early 1500s, a Dominican missionary and historian, Bartolomé de las Casas, a Spaniard himself, strongly

Explorers, right, watch Native Americans performing a spring ritual. The Natives sacrifice their largest horse, turn it toward the sun, and pray. Spaniards condemned the rituals, calling them pagan and misunderstanding their earthly significance.

disapproved of the Spaniards' inhumane treatment and capture of the Caribbean Indians, calling it "wholly unjustifiable." He wrote:

> [The Spaniards] made bets as to who would slit a man in two, or cut off his head at one blow; or they opened up his bowels. They tore the babies from their mothers' breasts by their feet and dashed their heads against the rocks. . . . They burned the Indians alive. . . . I saw all the above things.

Other influential Spaniards, such as Vasco de Quiroga and the Jesuits of Paraguay, shared Las Casas' beliefs. The

Hapsburg Emperor Charles V agreed that the Indians were being treated unjustly and inhumanely. He reformed the laws and abolished *encomienda* (taxation of Indians) in 1542. Unfortunately, public outcry brought back the *encomienda*, but by 1572 stricter laws prevailed and the Spanish Conquest was over.

Las Casas believed that the Spaniards' cruel treatment of the Native Americans set a policy for their future mistreatment. Whether this is true or not, most other European settlers took it upon themselves to be cruel and unfair to the native populations. They are responsible for their own cruel and unfair treatment of the Indians.

While many Spaniards were coming up from Mexico across North America, other Spaniards were invading the Southwest, home of the pueblo Indians (Zuni, Hopi, Acoma, and others).

HOPI TRIBES

The Hopi settled in Utah, Colorado, New Mexico, and Arizona. Modern Hopi have settled mainly in Arizona. Their peaceful nature and their spiritual inner pact to be peaceful made them easy marks for the Spanish, starting around 1540. Soon Spanish missionaries came to convert the Hopi to Christianity and to transform their lives. These Christians believed that all Hopi beliefs were erroneous and that such heathen natives needed to be "saved." Hopi resistance was not understood. Many Hopi were forced to become laborers, building churches and working for the Spanish. They were severely punished or killed for refusing to become Catholics.

In 1680, pueblo tribes joined together and drove the Spaniards out of the Southwest. But the Spanish would return and later converted some of the Hopi to Catholicism. This sparked a deadly attack of traditional Hopi against the

Progressivists. In 1700, the Traditionalists attacked the Awatovi pueblo in the dead of night, burning and destroying it. Over 700 men, women, and children died—both Christian and non-Christians—Indian against Indian.

The next white invaders arrived in 1826. These invaders were not conquerors like the Spanish, but explorers and hunters, who left the Hopi pretty much to themselves.

As years went by, the U.S. Government found that they couldn't control the Hopi or push them elsewhere, so they tried to break their culture by removing the children and sending them to boarding schools far from home. This was cruel treatment. Eventually, the government established a Hopi Reservation in 1882—one tenth of the land that the Hopi claimed. The U.S. Government also redrew the boundaries of the Hopi reservation in 1934, 1943, and 1977—each time making Hopi land smaller.

CALIFORNIA COAST TRIBES

In 1542, the Spaniards arrived in their galleons (heavy square-rigged sailing ships) and met the Indians of the California Coast. These mariners were wearing armor and carrying weapons. They wanted to find a suitable harbor to supply and refit their ships as they advanced between Mexico and the Philippines.

After other settlers threatened their dominion among the native peoples, the Spanish attempted to establish missions. Missions were communities in which the Indians were forced to live and work, where they were taught trades, such as blacksmithing and candle making. The first mission wasn't established in California until 1769 because of the difficulty of converting the Native Americans. After that, mission settlements dotted the California coast from San Diego to San Francisco.

Many Indians did convert to Catholicism, but some rebelled. They poisoned the priests, burned churches, and generally waged small bloody wars against the Spanish. In 1769, the Santa Barbara Mission in California, for example, reported 4,000 killed.

The "mission" Indian became an important but unwilling labor force for the Spanish. All the natives' religious expressions were forbidden, and Catholicism was taught by Spanish priests. Establishing missions had another advantage for the Spaniards. It would prevent English Protestants from exerting their influence.

The Mission Period lasted only 65 years but succeeded in almost totally destroying the Indian cultures of California. From being naked, the Indians were clothed; from being hunters and gatherers, they cultivated farms; from speaking their own language they learned Spanish; from following their own mystic-nature-based spiritual beliefs, they became Christianized. They lived in crowded communities and suffered lethal epidemics.

In 1834, the Mission Period ended, but things didn't improve for the Indians of California. The government promised land grants but never delivered them. The Indians had become dependent on the Spanish padrés (priests) and had to scratch for low-paying jobs as ranch hands, or they were allowed to live on governments land tracts. The Spanish had also introduced them to a poor diet and to alcohol, which proved harmful to them.

The California tribes had no culture or group to return to after the missions dispersed, and many became homeless. California was annexed by the United States in 1846, and more white settlers streamed in, further diluting Indian culture. Cultures of the Indians of Southern California no longer exist; possibly no more than a few hundred are living today, including those of mixed blood.

Christian missionaries invaded the Southwest where they built mission churches. Some Native Americans embraced the new religion brought to them by the missionaries and became Christians. Unfortunately, when the missionaries moved on, the Native Americans were often left with very little of their original culture.

The California Indians who met up with the Spanish were conquered because they couldn't imagine what the white man was after. They didn't understand single-minded passion for gold and the strong desire to proselytize and convert. If they could have imagined such motives, they would have been better able to protect themselves.

The Spanish Europeans dominated colonization in the New World and monopolized exploration of native peoples for 200 years. They caused loss of lives and loss of culture. They also introduced the most deadly force of all—disease.

DISEASE COMES TO THE NATIVE PEOPLES

In 1513, when Ponce de Léon and his group of Spanish explorers first arrived in Florida, they brought with them smallpox, chickenpox, cholera, typhus, influenza, and tuberculosis. The results were devastating. After the native populations began to have contact with the Europeans, disease and ill health pursued them relentlessly. Diseases that commonly plagued them were typhoid fever, cholera, measles, diphtheria, and especially smallpox.

Smallpox also killed many Indians in the Atlantic coastal areas. During a severe smallpox epidemic from 1584 to 1620, about 90% died among those who had survived an earlier epidemic. The loss of life was so great that when the pilgrims arrived from England in 1620, they offered thanks to God because so many Indians had been cleared from the land. They considered the native population a hindrance to their settling in the New World.

> Smallpox was the captain of the men of death in that war, typhus fever the first lieutenant, and measles the second lieutenant. More terrible than the conquistadors on horseback, more deadly than sword and gunpowder, they made the conquest . . . a walkover as compared with what it would have been without their aid. They were the forerunners of civilization, the companions of Christianity, the friends of the invaders.

How could disease have so severely devastated a strong and healthy people? Here's why.

The first immigrants to North America came in groups and spent many, many years in the frigid zones of Alaska before migrating farther south. This toughened those who survived—their bodies underwent a "cold filter." In other words, disease and germs became locked up in the frigid environment. The immigrants hunted and stayed in small groups or tribes. This kept them from widespread exposure to disease from humans. Moreover, they did not domesticate any of the animals in their environment. Thus, they avoided exposure to disease from animals, since even domestic animals can bring diseases such as smallpox and measles to humans. Because the Indians had not been exposed to many serious diseases, they had no natural immunity to them.

When the white man arrived, the natives were strong and healthy. Many historians believe that the populations who lived in North and South America before Columbus were disease-free. A Maya Indian compared health conditions before and after the Spanish arrived:

> There was then no sickness; they had no aching bones; they had then no smallpox; then had then no burning chest; they had then no abdominal pain; they had then no consumption [tuberculosis]; they had no headache. At that time the course of humanity was orderly. The foreigners made it otherwise when they arrived here.

However, some researchers doubted the Native Americans' supposed disease-free state, so they decided to examine the remains of pre-Columbian skeletons. They were able to determine that these early populations *did* have disease, especially tuberculosis, dysentery, parasitism, and respiratory diseases. Still, the diseases that white settlers brought to them were more devastating because the Indians had no natural immunity to them. In the New World, wherever the white man went, the native population decreased drastically. Haiti, for instance, went from 200,000 in 1492 to 29,000 in 1514.

The early Europeans brought disease to the Native American peoples, but many historians believe that Columbus and other Europeans brought disease back to Europe from the New World. One theory is that the spread of syphilis, a sexually transmitted disease, was caused by the voyagers coming back from the New World. Not everyone agrees with this theory; some believe that the rapid spread of syphilis was caused by a mutation of an existing disease in Europe.

THE TOLL OF DISEASE

Here are a few examples of the devastation that befell the Indians after the white man brought disease:

- Disease afflicted entire Natchez villages of native peoples, killing thousands. In 1662, French settlers first met the Natchez. By 1731, they destroyed the Natchez villages by wars and disease.

- The Pueblo Indians (e.g., Hopi, Zuni, and Acoma) were in northeastern Arizona, western New Mexico, and central New Mexico. In 1540, when Coronado (Don Francisco Vásquez de Coronado) arrived, there were about 70 Pueblos. Now there are no more 30. Nevertheless, of all the North American Indians, no group has preserved their culture and traditions to the extent that the Pueblo Indians have. Pueblo villages look very similar to the way they looked when Coronado first arrived.

- When smallpox and other diseases moved west to the northern Plains in 1781, more than 50% of Blackfeet died. Another plague of disease in 1857 killed more than 60% of those survivors.

- In the Great Plains, Native Americans such as the Mandan tribe who traded with the whites were felled by disease because of their association with whites. By 1837, only 125 of 3,600 Mandans were left.

- The tribes of the Great Basin (Utah, California, and Colorado) suffered greatly from the white man's diseases. Cholera alone killed 2,000 Basin tribes. The Nez-Percé, for example, lost many to disease, especially smallpox. It was the same in the Northwest.

The Navajo of the southwest were more fortunate because they weren't exposed to as much disease as other tribes. They were relatively isolated from other tribes and from each other. The Navajo Reservation today is the largest in the country.

Disease affected the Native American in another way. Medicine men lost the respect and prestige of their people because they couldn't cure the white man's disease, which felled so many members of their tribes. Much of Indian medicine up to that time was based on sweat baths and sweat lodges and cold plunges into a river or stream. These methods proved successful before the arrival of devastating diseases such as smallpox. But victims of smallpox would die from undergoing the sweat bath and cold dip.

When the English settlers arrived in the 1620s, there were about 1 million Indians living in North America, 500,000 of them on the East Coast. These natives of America could have made life difficult for the outnumbered pilgrims. The English might easily have left the New World if they feared for their safety and believed that they couldn't make a good life for themselves. But the Native Americans believed the colonists came in friendship, and they didn't protect themselves. Nor did

Diseases brought to the New World by white settlers didn't affect the Navajos as much as they did many other tribes. Many Navajo survived because their tribes stayed relatively isolated.

they know that a new enemy—disease—would cause so many to die.

These "new" diseases would eventually cause many Native American tribes to die out completely, and those who did survive were weakened by disease.

3

Resentments, Conflicts, and Wars in the Great Basin and Plateau

THE GREAT BASIN

Parched by the sun with a scant food supply, the Great Basin is a vast desert unkind to human life. The rugged Sierra Nevada mountain range keeps the Great Basin dry by blocking most of the rain clouds from moving east. It mainly covers what is now Nevada and Utah.

Still, the native populations (mainly Paiutes, Utes, Shosone, and Washo) adapted well to the harsh climate and terrain. They spent most of their time gathering food to keep from starving. Always on the move in search of water, edible plants, and small animals, the Great Basin tribes knew where to find food sources and when to move on. By persistence and good

The area known as the Great Basin covered mostly Nevada and Utah. The Paiutes, Utes, Shosone, and Washo tribes thrived there.

survival skills, they kept themselves fed, even through harsh winters. They were always thankful for the food and water that they had:

> The people realized they were part of nature, not masters of it, and they always remembered to share what they had with all of creation, leaving something—a bead or a stone—in exchange for each root they dug from the earth. They said prayers of thanksgiving when they drank life-giving water from a stream and thanked the spirit of the mountain when they gathered piñon nuts from the trees that lined the mountain slopes.

The nuts of the piñon pine were very important for the survival of the Great Basin tribes. " . . . The pine nuts belong to the mountain so we ask the mountain for some of its pine nuts to take home and eat." (Traditional Paiute pine nut prayer). But their life-giving trees were to face a cruel blow.

In 1776, the Spanish explored the southeastern area of the Great Basin and did some trading with the Shoshone. In 1848, white settlers and gold prospectors rushing to California disrupted the lives of these desert dwellers. Ten years later, Virginia City, Nevada, had become an urban center. Settlers chopped down the life-sustaining piñon trees for fuel and trampled seed plots. Ranchers kept taking more land, and many of the Shoshone and Utes were near starvation, begging for food. Disease moved in with the wagon trains, and 2,000 Indians of the Great Basin died of cholera. Some fighting erupted, but the tribes didn't persist because they knew they were outnumbered. In 1863, without even a treaty the U.S. government placed the Indians on reservations. Neither the government nor the white settlers realized or took it upon themselves to learn that they had placed in great jeopardy the very day-to-day existence of the desert-dwelling peoples of the Great Basin.

THE PLATEAU

The Plateau was a bounteous place to live. The Plateau region (mainly the Washington, Oregon, and Idaho areas) had great natural beauty, with trout-filled lakes, streams where salmon spawned, grassy plateaus, beautiful mountain borders, and abundant grazing lands for horses and cattle. The land covered the Columbia and Fraser River basins and included western Montana, eastern Washington, and north-eastern and central Oregon

NEZ-PERCÉ TRIBE

The tribes of the Plateau were actually made up of a variety of cultures. One of these tribes was the Nez-Percé (meaning pierced nose and pronounced něz purse). The Nez-Percé called themselves *Numipu*, "we people." As often seen with Native American tribes, the name they called themselves was different from the name by which they came to be known. The story goes that French settlers saw one native with a pierced nose and decided to characterize the whole tribe as "pierced nose."

Men and boys of the Plateau tribes hunted and fished. Women and girls gathered herbs, berries, and roots, wove baskets and mats, and made clothing. The Nez-Percé became excellent horse breeders and often traded their horses for the horses of travelers on the Oregon Trail. In time they became excellent breeders of Appaloosa horses. The tribe's work with horses spurred them to create

The Nez-Percé tribe, so called because some members had pierced noses, adorned their horses with elaborate riding gear.

decorated horse gear, and they wore elaborate beaded shirts and riding clothes. The Nez-Percé also did much trading with Plains Indians and other Plateau tribes.

Each autumn and spring, the Nez-Percé crossed the Bitterroot Mountains to hunt buffalo in eastern Montana.

They happily returned each winter to their sheltered valleys in the Plateau. The tribe loved their land in the Plateau because of their Earth-Mother–based religion and because it was the homeland of their forefathers. They had a good life.

About 1805, the Lewis and Clark Expedition arrived in the Plateau with their Indian guide, a Shoshone woman named Sacajawea. The Nez-Percé Indians greeted the explorers warmly. They trusted the explorers and gave them presents and cama root (starchy root of a variety of lily). Cama root, eaten in various forms, cooked or raw, was a staple of the Plateau Indians' diet. The Lewis and Clark explorers did not try to manipulate the Indians. They assured the Indians that they had come in peace for the purpose of exploring and mapping the land between St. Louis, Missouri, and the Pacific Ocean.

When the Lewis and Clark explorers canoed into the Rockies with the help of Sacajawea to find river routes for them, they left their horses and saddles with the Nez-Percé for safekeeping. When the weary travelers returned in the spring, their horses and belongings were returned to them in good condition. The spirit of cooperation and friendship that the white men and the Indians showed was a rarity during the years of exploration and white settlement. The Nez-Percé respected the explorers because they didn't try to force them to buy furs, to teach them about the white man's religion, or to "plow up Mother Earth for farms."

Although Lewis and Clark treated the Nez-Percé people fairly and in a friendly manner, their explorations were aimed at claiming the land of the Oregon Territory for white settlers. In the end, this meant displacing the Indians from their land. So this friendship in the end benefited only the white man.

In the early 1800s after they obtained horses, the tribes of the Plateau settled into a brief period of peace and prosperity. Unfortunately along with the prosperity came less desirable things. Disease brought by white men and passed among the tribal peoples wiped out many of the Plateau tribes starting in the late 1700s. From 1829 to 1832, almost all of the Chinook tribe died from disease that the white settlers brought. More and more Europeans kept arriving, many settling in the Washington and Oregon territories. More disease.

Over the years after the Lewis and Clark Expedition arrived, the Nez-Percé, by means of treaties with the whites, were repeatedly forced to give up their land to the government. Eventually, the Plateau peoples became boxed in by the whites. Starting in 1843, the Washington territorial governor Isaac Stevens threatened and bribed the Indians into signing a succession of 52 treaties in which they ceded (gave up) their lands. By forcing them into reservations, he gained 157 million acres of Plateau Indian territory. In 1855, a treaty was supposedly made that promised certain lands to the Nez-Percé. The Indians believed that the treaty was binding. They were wrong. The treaty was worthless, because the Senate never ratified (approved) it.

Meanwhile, white settlers took the Powder River country, Black Hills, and one third of the remaining Sioux reservation. The Plateau tribes were starting to be crowded out.

Soon many greedy white miners arrived to the Plateau looking for gold. This led to the bloody Yakima wars of 1856 to 1858, which spread all the way to the Pacific Coast. In 1861, gold was discovered on an Indian reservation in Idaho. Hordes of miners (5,000 to 10,000) flowed into Idaho, but the government turned a deaf ear to the Indians' pleas to get rid of the white miners. However, the government did make a treaty with the Indians promising to send them supplies. Being mostly confined to a reservation made the Nez-Percé dependent on the government for many supplies. For a while, the government did send goods to compensate the Indians for ceding their land. However, often the goods arrived damaged or in a lesser quantity than promised. In 1862, during America's Civil War, the government stopped sending these supplies because they diverted all their efforts to the Civil War. Helping the Native Americans was no longer important—if it ever was.

By 1876, Native Americans had no real independence. The Nez-Percé tribe, forced from their lands, fought battles against the white settlers and even defeated them for a time. The most memorable war was the four-month Nez-Percé war (Chief Joseph's Retreat).

CHIEF JOSEPH'S RETREAT

Chief Joseph was a warrior, diplomat, and powerful but peaceful chief, who was finally provoked into fighting white troops. He and some other Nez-Percé tribesmen refused to cede any more land to the government. With 750 warriors from many bands, Chief Joseph waged the Nez-Percé War. For four months in 1877, the tough Nez-Percé outwitted 3,000 soldiers and led them in chase over 1,600 miles across Oregon, Idaho, Wyoming, and Montana, almost to Canada. The white soldiers pursued with orders to kill all Indians, including women and children. This routed many more Indians to flee to "Indian Territory" (Oklahoma and Arkansas), where malaria was rampant.

It was a hard four months. Tired and worried about his people and about to be captured, a dejected Chief Joseph

Nez-Percé Chief Joseph led his tribe into battle with white settlers. The 750 Nez-Percé led 3,000 settlers in a chase across the Northwest. Eventually the respected chief grew weary of fighting.

surrendered after the last battle of Bear Paw Mountain with these sorrowful words:

> I am tired of fighting. Our chiefs are killed. Looking Glass is dead. It is cold and we have no blankets. The little children are freezing to death. My people, some of them, have run away to the hills and have no blankets, no food; no one knows where they are—perhaps freezing to death. I want to have time to look for my children and see how many I can find. Maybe I shall find them among the dead. Hear me my chiefs. I am tired; my heart is sick and sad. From where the sun now stands, I will fight no more forever.
>
> *Surrender speech of*
> *Nez-Percé Chief Joseph, 1877*

In the end, the whites outlasted Chief Joseph and his band and took their land.

4

Resentments, Conflicts, and Wars on the Northwest Coast and in the Southwest

NORTHWEST COAST

A narrow strip of land extending from the Gulf of Alaska to the Chetco River in Oregon was home to the native peoples of the Northwest Coast. Remarkably, many different tribes (e.g., Chinook, Belle Coola, Kwakiutl, Squamish, and Tlingit) with at least 45 languages shared a common culture. The Northwest Coast had an abundance of food sources on sea and land. The native peoples didn't take this gift of abundance for granted and honored the spirits of the fish and animals that they ate.

Starting in 1741 when the first Europeans discovered the Northwest Coast, the Northwest peoples began trading sea otter pelts for iron tools and firearms. These white men didn't try to

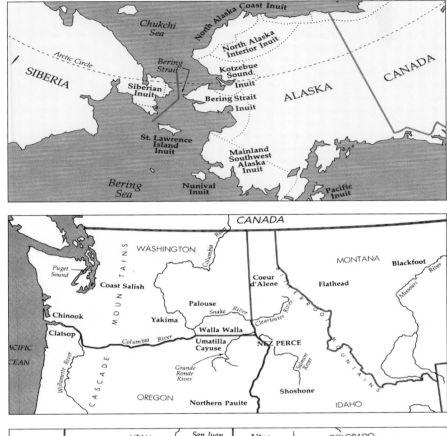

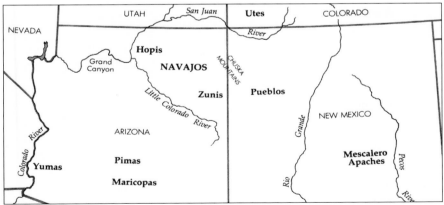

The Chinook, Belle Coola, Kwakiutl, Squamish, and Tlingit tribes lived on the northwest coast from Oregon to Alaska and in the Southwest.

change or convert the Indians. They only wanted them to keep supplying furs. So the Northwest Coast Indians and the white traders had a harmonious relationship. But it didn't last. The traders soon wanted to settle in this beautiful land with its oceans and rivers filled with salmon, trout, seals, and whales, and its mountains and forests populated with goats, deer, bears, and elk. This meant, as in other parts of America, pressuring the Indians to give up their land.

WARS AND POTLATCH

The activities of the Northwest Coast tribes centered mainly around two things: wealth and status. Indians attained wealth from the riches that the land and sea had to give them. They also acquired wealth and possessions by successfully trading with white settlers.

Wars were an outgrowth of the value system of the Northwest Coast tribes and were also part of their culture. Tribes warred against each other from the Northwest Coast to the California Coast to gain more lands and acquire more wealth. They took captives and forced them to become slaves to wealthy, high-ranking Indians. Slaves were made to do back-breaking work and to provide proof of their owners' status and wealth. They were often killed by their owners at a potlatch ceremony, or, according to tradition, after a family built a new home, when their bodies were placed in the ground under carved door totem poles.

At the root of the Northwest Coast Indian culture was the *potlatch* (Chinook meaning "to give")—as unique to the Northwest Coast peoples as were their beautifully carved totem poles. The potlatch was a ceremony of gift giving and receiving from one clan to another. The potlatch ceremony fostered good and friendly relations with another lineage of the same tribe. Preparation for this feast of giving and receiving

A Native American wearing traditional potlatch dress. This ritual focused on gift giving and feasting. The tribe member with the highest status received the most lavish gifts.

took years. Because people placed great value on wealth, the more a clan house had to give the more status the clan had.

The potlatch began with massive and elaborate feasting, and gift-giving continued for as long as 12 days. Every guest received gifts—the more status a person had the better gift they received. A high-ranking guest might have received a canoe. A lower-ranking guest might have received a cedar blanket.

The potlatch custom continued for many years, but even this tradition was changed by the whites. The white settlers bartered so many furs, mass-produced blankets, and other goods that the Indians acquired much wealth. As a result, the potlatch became competitive and lost its spiritual meaning. By the mid-1800s, the potlatch had become a caricature of itself—an overdone ceremony aimed at embarrassing and humiliating rival clans. Another reason for this change was the white settlers' strong disapproval of warfare among tribes and clans. Warfare did cease, but the potlatch became an outlet for the Indians' aggression.

Christian missionaries opposed the potlatch and in 1884 talked the government of Canada into outlawing it. Still, the Northwest Indians held their ceremonies in secret. As a Kwakiutl chief said regarding the potlatch and about the whites' attempt at dominance:

> We will dance when our laws command us to dance . . . we will feast when our hearts command us to feast. Do we ask the white man, "Do as the Indian does?" It is a strict law that bids us dance. It is a strict law that bids us distribute our property among our friends and neighbors. It is a good law. Let the white man observe his law, we shall observe ours.

In 1951, the Canadian law against potlatch was thrown out, and the tradition of potlatch was restored.

Native Americans saw the totem poles as spiritual guides, but Christian missionaries saw them as evidence of heathen activity.

Christian missionaries arrived in the Northwest, as in California (see Chapter 2). Their "mission" was to teach English and other skills to the Indians and to make the Indians give up their traditions. They misunderstood the Indians' attachment to their beautifully carved totem poles. The missionaries believed that the Indians worshipped their totems. They were wrong. The Indians viewed their totem poles as spiritual guides.

SOUTHWEST

See Chapter 2 for information about the Hopi Tribe and the Mission Period.

Apache Tribe

In 1540, the Spaniards met up with the Apaches—a strong-willed people, not to be forced into anything. The Spaniards promised the Apaches peace, but they broke their promise. So the Apaches attacked. For 300 years, hostilities flared between Spanish and Apaches, with whites kidnapping Indians for the slave trade. Apaches also kidnapped and raided other tribes, such as the Pawnee. They stole horses from the Pueblo Indians and became even fiercer raiders with the help of horses. By 1650, the Apaches were in open warfare with the Spanish.

Later, the growing stream of European white settlers to the Southwest provoked the Apaches. *Apache Wars* persisted on and off from 1846 to 1868 and were targeted against the miners who were advancing into New Mexico and Arizona. Soon the besieged miners asked the U.S. government for help and protection. And so the Apaches had another foe.

In Arizona, Cochise and Mangas Coloradas (Red Sleeves) from different bands of the Apache tribe fought the U.S. government to keep miners away from Apache lands. In 1862, they attacked the California militia on their way to New Mexico at what is now called Apache Pass. At about this time, the Apache joined forces with the Navajo. Meanwhile, General "Gentle Jimmy" Carleton ordered all Apache and Navajo to be shot on sight. It was war.

In 1863, the government, intimidated by Mangas Coloradas's leadership abilities, invited Colorodas to a peace parley. He never came back alive. The Apaches reported that Mangas Coloradas was murdered. The government stated that he tried to escape and they killed him. After that, many Apaches ran south to Mexico to avoid being put in prison. Those who didn't escape were marched 350 miles to Bosque Redondo upon orders of the government. This travesty was called *The Long Walk.* In 1876, the government tried to relocate the Apaches to San Carlos Reservation. The Apache leader Geronimo refused. More Apache Wars. Still, many Apaches did settle in San Carlos.

In 1885, Geronimo led a small band of Apaches into the Arizona and Mexico mountains. General Crook, the commander of the army in Arizona, understood the Indians' grievances and unfair treatment and said so. He fought Geronimo for months and finally persuaded him to surrender. Geronimo surrendered on the condition that after two years he and his tribe could return to the San Carlos Reservation. During the two years, Crook's superior was General Sheridan, commander in chief of the army. Sheridan persuaded President Grover Cleveland to reinstate the former army policy toward the Indians. "The only good Indian is a dead Indian."

So President Cleveland recommended that Geronimo be hanged, and he had the other Apaches sent to Fort Marion Prison in Florida. Many died in prison under harsh conditions in a climate they weren't used to. Their children were taken from them and sent to Carlisle Indian School in Pennsylvania. More than 50 children died there, and only a few of those who lived ever saw their families again.

The famous chief Geronimo was an Apache. Members of the Apache tribe worked with the army hoping to be rewarded, but they ended up in a Florida jail instead.

Some Apaches had worked for the army thinking they would be rewarded for this. They had led the soldiers to Geronimo and to the other Apaches who fled. Even the Apaches who helped the whites and betrayed their own tribesmen were sent to prison in Florida. There was no reward for their cooperation, only punishment. General Crook, in protest to this cruel maneuver, resigned from the army.

Navajo Tribe

The Navajo and Apache started migrating from Canada around 1300 and arrived in the southwest around 1500. The Navajo Reservation of today is 16 million acres—the largest Indian reservation in the United States. It extends into parts of New Mexico, Arizona, and Utah.

The Navajos lived in small family groups apart from other tribes and from each other. This way of life protected them from measles, influenza, and smallpox, which killed many Indians across the country.

The Navajos learned to capture horses from the Spaniards. They also stole sheep, cattle, and weapons. They even stole cattle from the American commander general in addition to many sheep and horses from ranches of settlers. They became so successful at stealing from the Spaniards that Spanish agents had to send to Europe for 1,500 additional horses. Navajo warrior skills prevented the Spanish from seeking retribution.

The U.S. government was determined to put a stop to the Navajo thievery of their livestock. They made treaties in which the Indians had to promise to stop stealing. Still, the stealing continued. The government didn't realize that the Navajo chiefs who signed the treaties were only local headmen and that they had no power over any other Navajo group.

In 1863, U.S. Colonel Kit Carson had orders to clear out the Navajos. He and his soldiers did this by destroying their source of food. They killed their livestock and burned their fields. They also committed more brutal acts. For example, army soldiers cut off the breasts of Navajo girls. After less

Navajos used their resources for making tools. They even learned to capture and tame horses from the Spaniards.

than one year of this torture, the starving Navajo survivors surrendered from their hiding place in Canyon de Chelly, New Mexico. The last 500 endured The Long Walk of 300 miles across difficult terrain in harsh weather to Fort Sumner in Bosque Redondo, New Mexico. Altogether, 8,000 Navajos made the journey. They were imprisoned from 1864 to 1868 in a wasteland of 40 square acres of flatland, where not even corn would grow. Many died on The Long Walk. Still more died in captivity.

By the fourth year of their captivity, the Navajos were in utter despair. That year, they signed a peace treaty with the government entitling them to 3½ million acres of land—half in New Mexico and half in Arizona. It took years to cultivate this land, which had been destroyed earlier, and they had to go back to hunting and gathering to survive. Adding to their difficulties was a long drought. By the 1880s, the government granted the Santa Fe Railroad the Navajos' best land. White settlers began crowding in on the Navajos, bringing alcohol and disease. Remarkably, over the years the Navajos thrived once more.

Resentments, Conflicts, and Wars in the Southeast and Great Plains

THE SOUTHEAST

The warm fertile lands bordering the Gulf of Mexico and the Atlantic allowed the natives who lived there to develop complex societies. These tribes built large temple mounds, created art, and built towns. They learned much about natural healing and remedies from nature. Nuts, berries, edible plants, and game animals were plentiful. They took up farming and were good at it. The peoples of the Southeast had no struggles against harsh climate or parched soil. But from the 1500s on, they did have struggles against white settlers pushing them west away from their rich and beloved homeland.

The Native Americans of the Southeast comprised peoples from

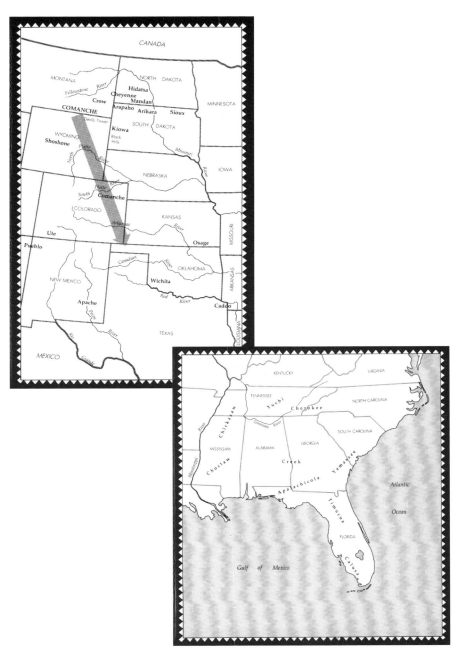

The areas bordering the Gulf of Mexico were home to the Choctaw, Chickasaw, Creek, Natchez, Seminole, Catawba, Cherokee, and Tuscarora tribes.

Louisiana, Mississippi, Alabama, Florida, Georgia, and the Carolinas. Most of the tribes were Choctaw, Chickasaw, Creek, Natchez, Seminoles, Catawba, Cherokee, and Tuscarora.

Natchez Tribe

The Natchez people have been called "People of the Sun." They believed in a Supreme God who lived in the sky. The Natchez society was well established for five centuries when the first Europeans—French—arrived in 1662. Between disease and warfare, the Natchez population had greatly decreased. The Spanish controlled Florida by the early 1700s. Spanish missionaries tried to convert the Indians to Christianity and forced them to work in the fields and supply food for the missions that they established. In addition, the British and a few French were moving farther southeast to establish new colonies. The Europeans captured the Indian and used them as slave laborers to clear the land and get it ready for cultivation. They also sold Natchez Indians to landowners far enough away that they couldn't find their way home. Many Indian families were broken up and never saw each other again. By 1731, the French had sold most of the Natchez survivors into slavery in the Caribbean. A very few escaped and joined the Chickasaw and Creek tribes.

Meanwhile, cotton became a prized crop, and cotton planters needed more land. They persuaded the Indians to cede their lands in exchange for removing their debts to white tradesmen. This was not a fair exchange.

Cherokee Tribe and the Trail of Tears

The Cherokee who were living in North Carolina used every means legally to hold onto their land. Even with 30 treaties, the Cherokees were losing their land piece by piece to the whites. Many whites sided with the Indians' right to keep their ancestral homeland. Still, state governments passed laws that took away Native American lands and their right to appear in court. The chief justice of the Supreme Court, John Marshall, declared these laws unconstitutional. But the Indians' old foe, Andrew Jackson, who was by then president of the United States, passed the Indian Removal Act in 1830. This forced the Cherokee and other tribes to move west of the Mississippi to a land unfamiliar to them.

From 1830 to 1838, a total of about 60,000 people of the Five Civilized Tribes (Cherokees, Chickasaw, Choctaw, Creek, and Seminole) moved—mainly walked—west.

In 1836, 13,000 Cherokees were forced to leave their homeland. Soldiers dragged many people out of their houses and set their houses on fire to make sure they couldn't stay or run away. The Cherokees carried with them whatever they could, leaving the rest of their belongings behind. Families became separated and never saw each other again.

The 1200-mile walk from the Great Smoky Mountains to the Indian Territory in Oklahoma was a *Trail of Tears*. Rain, wind, and snow followed the travelers. Their blankets were wet, and they wrapped pieces of blanket around their feet to prevent frostbite. Cholera and measles dogged them. About one quarter of the Cherokees died along the way. But their suffering didn't end when they reached Oklahoma. The western tribes already living there resented them and killed many more.

Some Indians never made the trip. They managed to escape and hide in different areas of Louisiana, Mississippi, North Carolina, Tennessee, Georgia, and Alabama. The United States finally gave a tract of land in Alabama to those few who stayed behind. This was too little, too late.

President Andrew Jackson forced 13,000 Cherokees to leave their homes in North Carolina. The natives walked 1,200 miles from the Great Smoky Mountains to Oklahoma. This removal is known as the "Trail of Tears."

Seminole Tribe

Most of the Seminoles hid in the swamps of the Everglades of Florida. Seminole means "runaway." These Indians were a blending of different tribes of the Southeast, especially the Creeks. General Jackson and his troops hunted down the Seminoles, raided, and burned their villages. In 1823, the government gave the

In 1861, with the beginning of the Civil War, the soldiers were pulled from the forts to fight in the war. Their replacements were volunteers, no match for the Indians. The Plains became a dangerous place for whites; livestock was stolen and soldiers' safety was in jeopardy. The situation became so bad that the army used Confederate soldiers on parole to guard the forts. Still, whites' superior weapons and greater numbers eventually prevailed over the Indians.

In 1878, the Cheyenne, who had already been banished from their homeland, returned and fought. Three hundred Cheyenne fought white soldiers with only 70 warriors. These fierce warriors won all four battles against the army. General Sheridan failed again and again to capture these Indians, who fled to Nebraska. Eventually, the Cheyenne were captured and badly mistreated. A few Indians escaped and were hunted down by white soldiers. When asked why he massacred these Indians, General Sheridan replied, "Why do you call it a massacre? A number of insubordinate cunning, treacherous Indians." He had no regard at all for the Indians as human beings. Of like mind, General Frederick Pitkin of Colorado said, "My idea is that unless removed by the government, they must be exterminated."

Little Bighorn (Custer's Last Stand)

In 1874, General George Armstrong Custer led an expedition into Lakota territory, breaking the treaties of 1851 and 1868. Nick-named Long Hair because of his long blond hair, Custer falsely claimed that there was "gold around the roots of the grass." This made white prospectors pour into Lakota land. First, the U.S. government tried to buy the land from the Sioux. The

Sioux refused because they considered the land sacred. So the government simply took most of their reservation, including the sacred site. Many of the Lakota Sioux left, and the U.S. Army headed by Custer went out to find them and bring them back. The Sioux gave Custer a new nickname, Chief of Thieves.

Meanwhile, more Lakota and some Cheyenne, as summoned by Chief Sitting Bull were gathering on the shores of the Little Bighorn River in Montana. Many warriors were followers of Crazy Horse, a distinguished Oglala Sioux chief. With 600 soldiers, Custer decided to attack the Indian warriors, even though he was out-numbered. The Indians killed Custer and his soldiers. Though the Plains warriors had won the battle of Little Bighorn, soldiers chased them and killed them or forced them into small reservations. The remaining band with Sitting Bull surrendered in 1881.

The reservation where the surviving Indians were forced to live was parched and impossible to farm. The food and supplies that the government was providing kept dwindling. They went hungry and became sick.

Wounded Knee

In 1889, a new spiritual movement spread among the Native Americans. It was called the Ghost Dance. This movement grew from a vision of Wovoka, a Paiute Indian, that a new age was coming for the Indians—a time when whites would disappear and the buffalo would return. The Ghost Dance arose partly because of white pressure to make the Native American abandon their customs and accept white customs. Part of this pressure included sending Plains Indian children away to boarding schools. The ghost movement gave the people hope for better days. It

Soldiers killed Sitting Bull, a Sioux chief, because they believed he headed the Ghost Dance movement. His death led to the Wounded Knee massacre.

spread quickly across the Great Plains, but it frightened the whites because they didn't understand it.

In 1890, soldiers tried to arrest Sitting Bull, thinking that he headed the Ghost Dance. They killed him and 14 other warriors. Then when Chief Big Foot led a band of Sioux to collect their goods, soldiers stopped them and took them to Wounded Knee Creek. The Indians did a Ghost Dance, which frightened the soldiers. One soldier tried to take away a rifle belonging to Black Coyote, a young deaf Sioux. A shot was fired accidentally. Then the fearful soldiers started shooting. When they were finished, the army's 7th Cavalry had killed about 300 men, women, and children. The Wounded Knee Massacre marked the last outright slaughter of Native Americans, a systematic case of genocide (killing or destruction of an entire people, race, or culture) of the Native American people. It put a brutal end to a long period of Plains Indian wars.

Dawes Allotment Act

In 1887, the Dawes Allotment Act (or Indian Allotment Act) broke up Indian reservations into 160-acre parcels for each family household. Leftover land was sold. This act was disastrous to the Native American population. They weren't all farmers, and many leased or sold off parcels to non-Indians. In 1900, Native Americans had only 77 million acres. By 1934, two thirds of reservation land were owned by non-Indians. The idea behind the Dawes Act was that the Indians would become farmers and assimilate into the white culture—in other words—disappear. This did not happen and only further damaged the Indians and their culture. Again, a great misunderstanding emerged between two cultures. As stated by anthropologist Peter Nabokov regarding the Dawes Act, it "probably created more widespread Indian suffering and left a more destructive legacy for Indians in the future than that infamous massacre [Wounded Knee]."

6

The Disappearing Buffalo

The swift decline of the buffalo is a story of misunderstanding, slaughter, and greed. The numbers put this story in perspective: up until the 1700s, there were 75 million buffalo roaming the continent of North America; by 1830, there were 40 million; and by 1890, the great American buffalo had become almost extinct. The story of the Plains Indians is the story of the buffalo.

A LOOK AT THE BUFFALO

The American buffalo (scientific name *bison*) is a huge and magnificent animal, weighing as much as 2,200 pounds and standing 6½ feet tall. Buffalo roamed freely in great numbers across the Great Plains of North America.

The massive buffalo of the plains became nearly extinct when the whites came to North America. The whites slaughtered buffalo faster than they could reproduce, thus depleting the supply of buffalo on which the Native Americans depended.

Buffalo are social animals, preferring to stay together and communicating constantly by snorting, groaning, and bellowing. In the Plains, they often gathered into large herds of several hundred. Sometimes, a stampede of bellowing buffalo thundered across the prairie, shaking the earth and crushing whatever lay in their path. These shaggy-haired beasts look awkward with their large rounded bodies and high-set humps, but their hooves are built to climb mountains and step easily over rocky terrain. In spite of their size, they are fast and can travel up to 35 miles per hour.

The Buffalo and the Plains Indians

The buffalo was most important to the native populations of the Plains because it literally sustained them. Native Americans greatly valued and respected not only the body of the buffalo but also its spirit. The buffalo played a role in Native American ceremonies, stories, dances, and songs. Native Americans remembered that for thousands of years the buffalo was the great provider for their ancestors. The buffalo of their ancestors was a giant buffalo, standing over 10 feet high with horns that measured 6½ feet across.

In the 1500s, horses that escaped from the Spanish conquistadors were roaming the Plains. Eventually, the native population learned to capture and then to ride the horses. Buffalo hunting became easier with horses because it was harder for the buffalo to escape. Horse and rider rode alongside a herd of buffalo and speared one animal, preferably through the lungs, or the hunter would use a bow and arrow to fell the buffalo. Many Indians used other hunting methods, such as wearing buffalo or coyote hides to confuse their prey and then to drive them into a canyon or swamp.

For the Plains tribes, especially the Blackfeet, Arapaho, and Cheyenne, the buffalo was their lifeline and their way of life. The buffalo meat fed them. The Indians made clothing, shelter, and tools with the rest of the buffalo. The tribes always celebrated after a successful buffalo hunt.

All year round, they told stories about the buffalo, or they had the buffalo playing a part in their stories. Blackfeet

On horse, many tribes developed more efficient ways of hunting buffalo.

children watched the buffalo's activities and movements and learned to become skilled hunters; from their elders they learned to be *respectful* hunters. For the Sun Dance in summer, the Blackfeet first cleansed themselves in a sweat lodge, then feasted on buffalo tongue. Often when an Indian hunter killed a buffalo, he rewarded himself by eating the buffalo liver—bloody and still steaming hot.

USES OF THE BUFFALO

Besides boiling and roasting the meat, Plains tribes made *pemmican.* They first dried the buffalo meat, then heated it and pounded it to a fine consistency. After adding buffalo fat, they packed the meat tightly into sacks made of buffalo rawhide. They then jumped on the meat sacks until the contents became solid. This high-protein food nourished them in winter and could be kept for up to 30 years.

After eating their fill and preparing the rest of the buffalo meat for later use, the Native Americans made use of the rest of the buffalo carcass. Not a scrap was wasted. They used buffalo rawhides (unsoftened hides) for tipis (tepees), drums, and bags. By working a mixture of fat, brains, and liver into the hide to soften it, they could make moccasins, clothing, and bedding. Blackfeet children made rattles from hooves strung on rawhide cords. Buffalo hair was used for ropes, headdresses, and dolls, and spinning tops were made from horns. For snowy weather, Blackfeet made toboggans out of rawhide and runners for sleds from buffalo ribs. Other bones became tools. The Indians respected, used, and didn't waste any part of the buffalo. Then came the Europeans.

THE RAILROAD AND BUFFALO BILL

In the 1800s, settlers from Europe moved across the Mississippi River and began to force the buffalo (and the native population) farther west. Eventually, they pushed the native tribes west allowing them no rights to live and use the land that they inhabited for many years.

The Great Plains was at that time a rough, undeveloped frontier. Workers were hired to build and lay railroad tracks across Plains Indian country. The Indians called these railroad tracks "iron tracks" or "iron horses," and they despised them because they were invading their homeland. The railroad workers needed to be fed, and the railroad company decided that buffalo meat would be the cheapest way of providing food for so many men. No one ever considered that the

When the government hired workers to help build railroads, they slaughtered buffalo for cheap meat with which to feed the workers. As a result, the buffalo supply rapidly diminished and the Native Americans were forced to find another means of sustenance.

buffalo was necessary for the Native Americans' way of life. So the railroad and the U.S. Army hired hunters to kill the buffalo to feed the workers.

Among the buffalo hunters, one young man, Bill Cody, stood out. He was already known for his brave and adventuresome spirit, when as a teen he delivered mail on horseback for the Pony Express through dangerous Indian territory. Bill's skill as a buffalo hunter far exceeded all the others. And he loved a challenge.

First, Bill chased a group of buffalo with his speedy horse, Brigham. Then he steered a group of buffalo by crowding his horse into the animal at the edge of the herd. The buffalo didn't scatter when they were being pursued; they continued to follow the leader. Bill got himself in position to aim at the buffalo's head, then shot. If he happened to shoot the leader of the herd—always a female—the buffaloes continued moving but didn't stampede. Eventually, Bill got the group of buffalo to move almost in a circle by crowding them with his horse. This way he was able to shoot and kill almost a small herd. He often killed a dozen buffalo in one day. In 18 months, Bill Cody killed 4,280 buffalo.

Ned Buntline, a writer of adventure stories, created an action hero named Buffalo Bill in his books. This character was based on Bill Cody. Because of this, people began to regard Bill Cody as a hero. They called him Buffalo Bill. The name stuck with Bill for the rest of his life.

Buffalo Bill, Buffalo Bill
Always aims and shoots to kill
He never missed and never will,
And the company pays his bill.

Still, Buffalo Bill didn't believe in killing buffalo without a purpose. Unfortunately, other frontiersmen did not feel the same way.

BUFFALO FOR SALE AND SPORT

People liked the taste of buffalo meat, and it came to be in demand in the Northeast. By the 1870s, people in the eastern states had learned new ways of treating hides and thus discovered more uses for them. Many frontiersmen later hunted buffalo for their prized skins alone. They

When the railroad steamed through the Great Plains, passengers would hang out the windows to shoot buffalo for sport. The carcasses were rarely used and often rotted in the sun.

took the skins to sell and left the huge carcasses to rot on the prairie. The numbers of buffalo were dwindling, but many still remained. In fact, the buffalo herds were still so large that they would cause a train to stop while they lumbered over the tracks. Train riders then took out their shotguns and shot at the buffalo for sport. Rarely did they load a buffalo carcass onto the train. Mainly, the buffalo were left to rot where they fell. Still worse, in 1868, the Kansas Pacific Railroad advertised round-trip tickets for

$10 to "sportsmen" to ride into buffalo hunting grounds to shoot at buffalo:

> An excursion train will leave Leavenworth, Kansas on Tuesday, October 27, 1868 for Sheridan, Kansas. Ample time will be had for the great Buffalo hunt. Buffalo are so numerous along the road that they are shot from the cars nearly every day.

Stench from the carcasses soon was everywhere. Within five years, 2½ million buffalo were killed in Kansas Territory. This was a tragedy for the buffalo and a tragedy for the Plains tribes.

WHITE EXPANSION AND WARS

In 1868, war broke out between the settlers and the native tribes in the Plains of Kansas because white settlements moving west of the Mississippi were intruding into the land that was the Indians' domain. The Sioux had already been having bloody fights over expansion of European settlers and frontiersmen into their territory. The Arapaho and Cheyenne went on the warpath as well over the buffalo slaughter. About 2,000 Native Americans fought federal troops. However, Sherman's attitude was to protect at all costs the new settlers crossing the Plains. He said of this war against the Native Americans: "The more we can kill this year the less will have to be killed the next war." General Grant, a candidate for U.S. president, agreed with this tactic. This attitude is well beyond misunderstanding; it is sheer brutality.

The European settlers felt that they could take the land because they viewed the Native American as uncivilized and heathen. Missionaries wanted them to stay on reservations but go to white schools and learn about the Christian God. They didn't want them to preserve their rich traditions. The white man didn't respect Native American cultural and spiritual values. The white man broke treaties with the Native Americans, raided their villages, and killed their people, even the papooses (babies). This made the native tribes fight back by attacking wagon trains, raiding white settlements, and killing railroad workers.

After the Civil War, the American government signed a treaty with the Sioux and Arapaho, in which South Dakota west of the Missouri River was set aside as reservation for the native tribes. The Native Americans could hunt in North Platte and the Bighorn and Republican River areas as long as the buffalo lasted. Red Cloud, chief of the Oglala Sioux, was successful in driving out the white man and securing the "territorial" settlement of the treaty. However, Red Cloud knew by this time not to trust the white man's promises and wondered how long this treaty would last. When someone asked him how one would become like the white man, he answered:

> You must begin anew and put away the wisdom of your fathers. You must lay up food and forget the hungry. When your house is built, your store room filled, then look around for a neighbor whom you can take advantage of, and seize all he has.

Through the 1870s and 1880s, the killing of the buffalo by whites continued, mainly as an opportunistic money-making venture. Settlers sold buffalo hides for $3.50 to $4.00 each and buffalo tongues for 50 cents each. Buffalo horns were also sought after. Soon, great hills of discarded buffalo bones dotted the prairie. Then white frontiersmen learned that they could sell bleached bones for $7.00 to $10 a ton to be made into fertilizer. By 1888, even the bones were gone, and almost all the buffalo were dead. At one time, there were 70 to 75 million buffalo on the Plains; by 1890, 1,000 buffalo were left. They were nearly extinct.

In spite of the battles and loss of land that the native people suffered, the disappearance of their lifeline, the buffalo, brought about the most crushing defeat to the Native American people. The result was that they had to depend on the government for shelter and food.

THE BUFFALO'S COMEBACK

In 1872, President Ulysses S. Grant established the first national park in the Yellowstone Valley of Montana— Yellowstone National Park. His goal was to protect the rich and beautiful lands in the valley and to establish a safe refuge for wildlife. Within Yellowstone, the last buffalo herd was later discovered. However, poachers were still killing the buffalo. In 1894, only 20 buffalo were found in Yellowstone. A law passed by Congress calling for fines and imprisonment of poachers proved helpful, but the herd was still small—only 23 head in 1902. At this point, two additional herds of buffalo from ranchers were introduced into Yellowstone to restore the herd. This gave the animals a good start in their comeback. Still it hasn't been an easy road.

By 1905, some Americans realized the importance of sharing our world with wildlife. The American Bison Society was formed, and a small herd was brought to a valley in Montana. More buffalo were added. By 1908, the buffalo population there rose from an initial 37 to 450 head of buffalo. Independent organizations and interested ranchers and farmers have also joined the movement to bring back the buffalo. As a result the American buffalo no longer faces extinction.

Still, there are many ranchers and farmers living near Yellowstone National Park who object to the buffalo in Yellowstone. They believe that some of the wild buffalo may be infected with a bacterial disease, brucellosis, which causes miscarriages in cattle. The ranchers worry that they will suffer losses to their cattle when any buffalo move outside the park. In spite of the fact that there has never been a documented case of brucellosis transmission from buffalo to cattle, ranchers are allowed to kill any buffalo that leaves Yellowstone Park. Native Americans and environmentalists oppose this, suggesting that the wandering buffalo be moved to native-owned lands for rebuilding their herds. Nevertheless, the state of Montana and the federal government still allow this practice of controlled buffalo hunting.

In South Dakota in 1991, more than 19 tribes created the Inter-Tribal Bison Cooperative (ITBC), an organization dedicated to the restoration of buffalo to both tribal lands and tribal life. Says Fred DuBray, a Cheyenne River Sioux and past president of ITBC, "We recognize the bison as a symbol of strength and unity." The ITBC believes that " . . . reintroduction of the buffalo to tribal lands will help heal the spirit of both the Indian people and the buffalo. . . . To reestablish healthy buffalo populations on tribal lands is to reestablish hope for Indian people."

7

Resentments, Conflicts, and Wars in the Northeast

"Welcome, Englishmen."

These were the first words the pilgrims heard when they came ashore at Plymouth Harbor in 1620. Chief Massasoit (Yellow Feather) and others of the Wampanoag tribe met and befriended the pilgrims. Unfortunately, the Wampanoags were the first to catch the diseases that the Europeans brought.

NORTHEAST TRIBES

Native Americans of the Northeast lived in and around New York, Pennsylvania, and the New England and Great Lakes areas. Southern New England was the home of the strongest and largest tribes at the time that the pilgrims came to Plymouth Rock.

Tribes of the Northeast Territory—states that would become New England—first met the European settlers. Tribes in that area varied greatly.

The native population was large and included many tribes: Micmac, Iroquois, Delaware, Huron, Shawnee, Kickapoo, Potawatomi, Ojibwa, Winnebago, among others. The native peoples mainly spoke Iroquois and Algonquin languages.

Starting in the 1500s before the English colonists arrived, the call for fur by the French fur traders and later other Europeans created an occupation for many Indians of the Northeast. They were paid well with sugar, flour, and other foods in return for beaver, mink, ermine, and other animal pelts. The quest for fur drove many Ojibwa (Chippewyan) and Iroquois west. However, many Indians became dependent on goods from white settlers and moved near trading posts. Some white traders introduced alcohol to the Indians, which harmed them physically and mentally.

European traders began to settle on the Atlantic Coast from 1600 to 1650. Both whites and Indians benefited in the early days of trading. The Indians received knives, fishhooks, and tools from the whites, which helped them in their hunting, fishing, and work activities. White settlers learned from the Indians how to hunt and survive the harsh winters. Later, Chief Massasoit and the Wampanoags taught the pilgrims how to cultivate corn. Algonquins gave them food. Such generous offerings saved the pilgrims from dying of starvation. In fact, the British settlement in Jamestown, Virginia (1607), owes its survival through the first winter mostly to the Powhatan tribe.

The pilgrims who came to the Northeast in the 1600s were English, Dutch, and some Swedish. They came to the New World not as fur traders but as seekers of religious freedom, gold, and other opportunities for wealth. They especially wanted to claim a piece of land as their own— for their children and their children's children. It is not surprising that the lands they desired were Indian lands. And they kept wanting more and more land.

In Virginia, white settlers took all the land along the James River. The Powhatan tribe was pushed inland and lost their fertile fishing areas. Resentful and angry, the Powhatans sent a fatal message. In 1622, they attacked the British settlers and killed 350 people with the tools they acquired from the British through trading. They pushed dirt in the mouths of some of the settlers to teach them a lesson *not to eat up the land*. Still, the whites continued to take the lands, believing that they were somehow benefiting the Indians by being there. In 1607, there were about 14,000 Powhatans in Virginia; in 1669, there were about 2,900 Powhatan and 30,000 English. The U.S. government eventually established reservations for the remaining Powhatans.

Under pressure, Chief Massasoit sold a large tract of land in Massachusetts to white settlers, but the Indians continued to hunt on that land. Captain Miles Standish (leader of the Massachusett colony) questioned the Indians about this. "Did we not buy this [land] . . . ?"

Massasoit answered, "[The Earth] belongs to everybody and is for the use of all. How can one man say it belongs to him only?"

The Indians didn't understand private ownership. They had no reason to; it was not their way of life to individually "own" land and not allow others on it. Again, there was a lack of understanding between the two cultures. As Tecumseh, a Shawnee, stated, "What. Sell land! As well sell air and water. The Great Spirit gave them in common to all."

The Iroquois Tribe

The Iroquois came to be known as the People of the Long House because of the long multifamily houses they lived in. Iroquois tribes lived near the Huron and the Susquehanna tribes, the nomadic Algonquins, and

The Iroquois lived in long houses. The large houses allowed extended families to live together under one roof.

other tribes. For the Iroquois, warfare against neighboring tribes was a way of life. They went out in war parties with tomahawks to kill and to take captives. They would "sneak up on the enemy like foxes, fight like lions, and disappear into the woods like birds." The Iroquois had a cruel and brutal streak and terrorized their victims with prolonged tortures. The Jesuit priest Father Le Jeune described what he saw of Iroquois torture:

> One must be there to see a living picture of Hell. The whole cabin appeared as if on fire; and athwart the flames and dense smoke that issued therefrom, these barbarians, crowding one upon the other, howling at the top of their voices with firebrands in their hands, their eyes flashing with rage and fury—seemed like so many demons who would give no respite to this poor wretch. They often stopped him at the other end of the cabin, some them taking his hands and breaking the bones thereof by sheer force; others pierced his ears with sticks which they left in them. . . . As soon as day began to dawn, they lighted fires outside the village to display there the excesses of their cruelty, to the sight of the Sun. There they began to burn him more cruelly than ever, leaving no part of his body to which fire was not applied at intervals . . . Therefore, a hand, and almost at the same time a third severed the head from the shoulders, throwing it to the crowd, where someone caught it to carry it to the Captain Ondessone, for whom it had been reserved, in order to make a feast therewith.

In spite of his brutal tendencies, the fierce Iroquois hunter was respectful of the spirit of the animal he was hunting. An Indian brave setting out to hunt a deer would first become "one with the spirit of the deer" to help him catch his prey. When he caught the deer, he quietly and respectfully thanked it. Before skinning the deer, he first prayed for the deer's spirit. In contrast, the whites kicked the deer to see if it was dead, then cut it up right away, "robbing the deer of all its dignity."

LEAGUE OF THE FIVE NATIONS

Starting in 1390, the Iroquois-speaking tribes of the Northeast formed The League of the Five Nations, a union of the fierce Mohawks, the Oneida, the peaceful Onondaga, the Cayuga, and the Seneca. Sparked by a vision of unity and peace by the Huron prophet, Deganawidah, the League handled intertribal relations and warfare against non-League tribes.

A Council of 50 sachems (tribal chiefs) from each of the five nations made up the governing body. The Council was thoroughly democratic. That is, every decision had to be reached unanimously. If one sachem didn't agree, the rest of the Council would argue the issue until the one man was won over or until all were won over to his way of thinking. Women could never be sachems, but they chose all successors among the tribesmen when a sachem died or did not carry out his duties properly.

White settlers later came to admire the League's social structure. Some historians believe that the League provided a model for the Thirteen Colonies of the United States of America. However, it more closely resembled the United Nations, since it did not deal with internal affairs, such as taxes and law enforcement. Although the Iroquois nations were united and gradually ceased warring among themselves, they still pursued warfare for many years. The League disbanded in 1783.

WARS OF THE NORTHEAST

From 1636 to 1637, the *Pequot War* broke out. The English colonists of Connecticut, with the Narrangansett

Indians of Rhode Island who were enemies of the Pequot tribe, attacked and killed over 700 Pequots, including women and children. They burned the Indian village of Mystic, took over Connecticut, and became the masters of the Indians who remained. In 1666, the Pequots were given 2,500 acres of reservation. By 1783, reservation land was reduced to 214 acres. The Pequots later sued to regain their land. In 1983, the U.S. Government granted the Pequots $900,000 in restitution. In 1986, the Pequots built a bingo hall and later a huge casino. This and other business ventures bring in much revenue for the Pequot nation.

The *Iroquois Wars* (1643 to 1701) were fought against French-allied tribes. The Iroquois attacked and fought the Hurons, the Chippewyan, and other tribes. Many Hurons were killed, and only those who ran into the forest escaped the slaughter. The Iroquois Wars took an especially terrible toll on the Hurons, who had already lost 10,000 to disease epidemics from 1633 to 1635. Some Hurons joined the Iroquois League, making the Iroquois even stronger. The Mohawks became head of the Iroquois League because they were such fierce fighters.

Many French traders were also killed during the Iroquois wars. Warfare finally ended with a peace agreement and a promise of neutrality toward the French and the English. This didn't help the position of the Native Americans, and English expansion continued with renewed vigor.

King Philip's War was an uprising against white expansion in Massachusetts in 1675. This war had nothing to do with a king in Spain, France, or any other part of Europe. King Philip was the name that the English gave to Metacomet, leader of the Wampanoag tribe who led the war. This time the Native Americans had many weapons on their side— guns and ammunition. Many English, including women and

Native Americans fought the Europeans with guns and ammunition in King Philip's War, named not for some European king, but rather for a Wampanoag chief whom the English dubbed, "King Philip."

children, were killed. The combined tribes (Narragansett and others) took some settlers as captives. Eventually, because of sheer numbers the English settlers defeated the Indian tribes. Some Native Americans fled across the country to tribes in the north, south, and west. Many were sold as slaves in the West Indies (Caribbean) or were made servants in New England homes. King Philip's War ended in 1676 with the beheading of Metacomet.

The *French and Indian War* (1754 to 1763) was really a war between the French traders and the English colonists in North America and Canada. Indians fought on both sides. Many sided with the French because they believed the traders were not interested in expanding and taking Indian lands. They were right. But the colonists were interested in taking over the whole country. In 1763, the French lost the French and Indian War, and English expansion continued.

During the *American Revolution* (1776) of the colonists against their mother country, England, a strange association developed. Four of the six (with the addition of the Tuscarora) Iroquois nations chose to side with the British troops. Both the British and the white colonists at times promoted torture of the enemy by Indian warriors. In other words, the whites used the Indians as "punishers" for the enemy. The Indians were indeed used unethically and immorally.

The picture of friendship in the 1600s between pilgrim and Native American in the Northeast has sparked an important holiday in the United States—Thanksgiving. For Native Americans, however, Thanksgiving has become a "National Day of Mourning."

The Lenni Lenape and William Penn of Pennsylvania

I have great Love and Regard toward you, and I desire to win and gain your Love and Friendship by a Kind, Just and Peaceful Life.

William Penn to the Lenni Lenape Indians

hile he finished his business in England, William Penn sent letters to the natives with passengers ship-bound for the New World. He also sent ahead his deputy-governor and cousin William Markham, his agent James Harrison, and others to make land purchases and pave the way of friendship with the Lenape.

LENNI LENAPE

For 100 years before the first European settlers arrived in Pennsylvania (Penn's woods), the Delaware Indians, who called

This decorative blanket belonged to the Delaware Indians, the Lenni Lenape, who lived along the Delaware River.

themselves Lenni Lenape (lĕ'-nee lĕ'-nah'-pay), "the true people," or "the real people," lived in forests that lined both the Pennsylvania and New Jersey sides of the Delaware River. Other clans of the Lenape lived along the Susquehanna River in southeastern Pennsylvania, in parts of New York, and farther down the Delaware River in what became the state of Delaware.

The Lenni Lenape lived mainly in villages in simple houses made of tree bark set on poles no taller than a man (according to William Penn). They ate mostly cereal grains, fish, game, and fowl. At most meals they ate corn, cooked and prepared in different ways and combined with different foods. The Lenni Lenape were advanced in cultivating grains, especially corn. In fact, they taught the colonists how to cultivate and prepare corn. Tribes in other territories did this, too. Corn has a long history of aiding in the survival of both the natives and the white immigrants.

> The development of corn by prehistoric Indians has been called the most remarkable achievement in agricultural history. Of all grains, corn is the most completely domesticated, being the only one that cannot sow itself or take care of itself.

The Lenni Lenape had had contact with the Dutch, Swedes, and Germans for about 75 years before meeting the English Quakers, but their culture remained intact. They had no language and used pictographs to depict events to help them remember. Unfortunately, outside forces would chip away at their culture, and it would almost disappear altogether.

Penn described the Lenape as both revengeful and generous and their physical appearance as:

> . . . generally tall, straight, well-built and of singular Proportions; they tread strong and clever, and mostly walk with a lofty Chin. . . . They grease themselves with Bears-fat clarified, and using no defence against Sun or Weather, their skins must needs be swarthy. . . .

The Lenni Lenape believed in the presence of spirits in all things. They believed in a god and in immortality. They

The Lenni Lenape Indians lived in houses made of tree bark. They ate both gathered and cultivated foods.

were not warlike and believed in the dignity and worth of all people. They had many things in common with the spiritual beliefs of the Quakers who came to Pennsylvania. The Lenni Lenape also revered and respected rattlesnakes and were not harmed by them. The Lenni Lenape couldn't understand the whites' "war" on rattlesnakes, since rattlesnakes have never declared war on the whites.

WILLIAM PENN, GOVERNOR OF PENNSYLVANIA

William Penn came to the New World to escape persecution for being a Quaker. He had already spent time in prison in England for his Quaker beliefs. King Charles II gave Penn a large land grant in the New World as payment for a debt owed Penn's father. It was up to Penn to colonize it and manage it—as governor. He advertised throughout Europe for settlers to buy land tracts and settle in a beautiful land with freedom of worship. However, most of the early settlers came from England. Penn wanted to establish trade and peacefully gain title to the land called Pennsylvania.

Quakers believe in equality, simplicity, and peace. A Quaker who practices these principles would be certain to treat the native inhabitants fairly and equally. William Penn did this. Other colonists treated the Indians as intruders; the Pennsylvania colonists treated them as neighbors. Other colonies "took" land from the Indians. William Penn "purchased" land from them.

Basically, the colonists of Pennsylvania respected the Indians' right of domain. The Dutch and the Swedes also recognized the rights of the Indians to the use of the land on which they lived. The English knew they had title to the land as granted by King Charles II, but they went through the motions, respectfully, of purchasing the land from the Lenni Lenape.

WILLIAM PENN AND THE LENNI LENAPE

The day when 38-year-old William Penn arrived on Dock Street in Philadelphia in 1682 was a day of excitement and celebration for both Penn and the Lenni Lenape.

> The Indians, as well as the whites, had severally prepared the best entertainment the place and circumstances could admit. William Penn made himself endeared to the Indians by his marked condescension and acquiescence in their wishes. He walked with them, sat with them on the ground, and ate with them of their roasted acorns and homony. At this they expressed their great delight, and soon began to show how they could hop and jump; at which exhibition, William Penn, to cap the climax, sprang up and beat them all!

Much of the friendliness of the Indians was because of the fair treatment by the Dutch and Swedes. Also, Penn's agents and his gifts and letters from England had paved the way for harmony with the Lenni Lenape.

Wampum Belt given to William Penn by the Lenape in 1682 symbolizes both the land purchases and the friendship of the Indians with William Penn.

The first land purchase from the Lenni Lenape was made by Penn's deputy governor, William Markham in 1681. The land was located in Bucks County along the Delaware River. After Penn arrived from England, he made 10 more land purchases. Boundaries were marked out, for example, as "two days journey with a horse" and "as far as a man can go in two days." That system worked for awhile.

The land purchase price varied according to what goods were available and the wants of the Indians. The following is a partial list of what the Indians received in payment for a particular land purchase:

40 white blankets

40 combs

40 kettles, 4 whereof large

200 awls

40 kersey [woolen] coats

Two handful fishhooks

60 shirts

5 small saws

20 pairs shoes

2 ankers tobacco [anker = 10 gallons]

40 axes

2 ankers rum

200 knives

2 ankers cider

40 pairs scissors

2 ankers beer

In late fall of 1682, William Penn met with the Lenni Lenape and representatives of other tribes in a treaty of friendship under the Shackamaxon elm tree. The "Great Treaty" cemented Penn's friendship with the Lenni Lenape and allowed Penn to purchase much of the territory of Pennsylvania from them. Penn often met with Lenni Lenape sachems in Philadelphia and in Pennsbury Manor, his country home in Bucks County—5 hours by boat (with 8 oarsmen) from Philadelphia. He gave the Indians presents and helped to solve problems. Penn often visited the Lenni Lenape at their homes.

William Penn reluctantly went back to England in 1683 to take care of business matters. He returned to Pennsylvania in 1699 to stay for good. Unfortunately, business problems again called him back to England in 1701. He fell ill there and never returned to his beloved Pennsylvania home.

1980 AND 1990 POPULATIONS OF SELECTED NATIVE AMERICAN TRIBES

TRIBE	1980 CENSUS	1990 CENSUS
Cherokee	232,080	369,035
Navajo	158,633	225,298
Sioux 1	78,608	107,321
Chippewa	73,602	105,988
Apache	35,861	53,330
Iroquois	38,212	52,557
Seminole 2	15,074	10,363

Data are based on a sample.
From U.S. Bureau of the Census, August 1995.

"bury the hatchet." The truth is that early on the white settlers did not have a system of traditions that were comparable to the strong traditions of the Indians. What they did have was a feeling of superiority over the Indians. With this attitude, they sought to mold the Native American to live like the white man. This provoked misunderstandings, resentments, and revenge. One thing led to another, and nothing led to peace. Today we are trying to remedy this. Native American tribes and environmentalists are bringing back the buffalo.

RESTORING THE BUFFALO

In the words of Sioux leader, Red Cloud, the buffalo is a "sacred gift" to the Sioux from the Creator. A Kiowa

Apaches wait for a train after being released from Fort Sill. Soldiers held the Native Americans as prisoners of war in the early 1900s.

elder states his connection with the buffalo more strongly, "I love the land and the buffalo, and I will not part with it. I want you to understand well what I say." The settlers in the New World never understood the meaning of the buffalo to the Native American.

In 1991, 19 tribes joined efforts to form the Inter Tribal Bison Cooperative. Today 40 tribes are at work to bring back the buffalo to tribal lands. Cheyenne, Crow, Navajo, Shoshoni, and Sioux are buying buffalo and learning to raise and manage them. They believe this will help restore the ecological balance of the Plains.

Buffalo have certain advantages over cattle because buffalo do not deplete and damage the land as do cattle. For example:

- Buffalo "crop" the grass when they graze and leave tall coarse grasses, which shelter mice, birds, and other small creatures. Cattle deplete the range by overgrazing.

- Buffalo dung fertilizes the soil. Cattle dung makes the soil acid.

- Buffalo hooves aerate the soil. Cattles' hooves pack down the soil.

- Buffalo meat is higher in protein and leaner than beef.

- The coarse shaggy hair of the buffalo catches and protects germinating seeds that blow or fall on the buffalo's thick winter coat. When the weather turns warm, the buffalo sheds its coat and the seeds along with it. The seeds then germinate in the soil or are transferred or eaten by birds.

RESTORING THE APPALOOSAS TO THE NEZ-PERCÉ

When the Nez-Percé surrendered to Colonel Miles in 1877, they gave up their 1,100 Appaloosa horses. This was a great loss, since much of the tribe's activity centered around the Appaloosa. In 1991, The Chief Joseph Foundation was established in Idaho. Its aims are to preserve Nez-Percé culture and to promote cultural pride and healing through activities centered around the Appaloosa. Its goal for the future was to create an Equine Center on the Nez-Percé reservation, where individuals, especially youth, can learn horsemanship and "experience the satisfaction and pride of owning and caring for their own Appaloosa."

In 1991, Bob Browning, an Appaloosa breeder from New Mexico, donated 10 mares to the Chief Joseph Foundation. By 1997, there were 70 Appaloosas and an educational program of horsemanship and studies, a "Mounted Scholars Program."

On the last weekend in July, the town of Joseph, Oregon, celebrates Chief Joseph Days. Each year, members of Chief Joseph's band of Nez-Percé come from their reservation in Washington State to join the celebration. In 1988, the tribe formed a Cultural Resources Program in an effort to preserve their language, history, and arts and crafts.

BLACKFEET CLASS ACTION SUIT

Of the many efforts of the Native Americans to restore their culture and recoup their money losses, Elouise Cobell of the Blackfeet Tribe in Montana, is a frontrunner. She filed a class action suit in 1996 against the U.S. government on behalf of all past and present Individual Indian Monies Trust beneficiaries.

As a result of the 1887 Dawes Allotment Act (see Chapter 5), Native Americans were given land allotments of 40 to 320 acres through the Bureau of Indian

Affairs. The "catch" was that the government was in charge of all business requiring leases for grazing rights, oil, gas, and minerals. This income was to be held in trust for each family. The Treasury Department was to send out checks. The checks never came. Years went by. The federal government turned a deaf ear. More years went by. Meanwhile, Elouise Cobell, who came from a house with no electricity or running water, was getting an education. She studied accounting and became treasurer of her tribe. Then she went to college, but she had to leave early to care for her dying mother. Still, she could intelligently pursue what her tribe wanted from the government. It took years.

Fifty-five-year-old Elouise learned about loss of money, cover-ups, and betrayal of trust. Billions in income had been lost from her tribe's funds. She writes, "After years of litigation, I think many of us are simply shocked at the government's shameful behavior in this case. This is our government, routinely stonewalling and lying to the Court, Congress and us about our money, which the government has been stealing from us for more than 100 years."

In 1999, Judge Royce Lambreth ruled that the U.S. Treasury and the Department of the Interior must reform the Indian trust system under court supervision. The next step is to determine how much is owed to the Native Americans. Estimates are from $20 to $40 billion.

MAKING AMENDS

In 1917, Native Americans were encouraged by the U.S. government to enlist in the Armed Forces. Over 10,000 enlisted. In 1919, those who served in the Armed

Elouise Cobell was part of the Blackfeet class-action suit against the U.S. government. The Blackfeet tribe claim that the government drilled for oil on Native American land without properly paying the tribe for its use.

Forces were granted citizenship. In 1924, all Native Americans were given the right to vote. A group who later distinguished themselves during World War II was the Navajo Marine "code talkers." They were a group of young Navajos who developed an unbreakable code based on their language. These Native Americans

Marines enabled the Marines to take Iwo Jima after a month-long struggle. In 1982, President Ronald Reagan declared a National Navajo Code Talker Day. In 2001, President George W. Bush awarded the Congressional Gold Medal to five original Navajo code talkers as well as the Silver Congressional Medal to the more than 300 surviving code talkers.

In 1924, the Pueblo Lands Act was set up to claims to pueblo lands.

In 1934, the Indian Reorganization Act (Wheeler-Howard Act) stopped the land allotment and enabled tribes to form business corporations and govern themselves. They also were allowed freedom of worship.

In 1944, over 40 tribes met and formed the National Congress of American Indians. This established the Indians Claims Commission in 1946 so that tribes could file claims directly against the U.S. Government.

In 1953, the government officially terminated 13 tribes and many other bands. This meant that they no longer had federally recognized status. This in turn meant that the federal government took away services and annuities (sums of money paid yearly). In 1970, President Richard Nixon ended the termination policy, and Native Americans had self-determination.

In 1972, a group of activists took over the Bureau of Indian Affairs under the Department of the Interior and formed the American Indian Movement demand better programs for Native Americans. This same group staged an occupation at Wounded Knee, South Dakota, to charge Richard (Dickie) Wilson, Chairman of the Pine Ridge tribal council, with corruption. An overblown display, this occupation proved that the Native American had not disappeared. Unfortunately, two Indian activists were killed, and one military man was paralyzed.

William Kien, 83, helped the United States communicate in code during World War II. Kien and his fellow "code talkers" used a Navajo language to transmit secret messages. In 2001, President George W. Bush held a ceremony to award the Congressional Silver Medal to 200 Navajo code talkers.

Today, casinos are bringing in income to the many tribes. But some Indians believe that gambling is in conflict with Native American values. Nevertheless, unemployment and poverty are common on Indian reservations.

Efforts at making amends for injustices to the Native Americans are only touched upon in this chapter. Many more are in play. Some measures are good; some have turned out to be harmful. At any rate, the rebuilding of a culture's status and independence after many years of conflict and suffering is not an easy road.

To be yourself in a world that is constantly trying to make you something else is the greatest accomplishment.

Ralph Waldo Emerson

10,000 to 12,000 B.C.	First immigrants arrive in North America from Asia
ca 1390	Iroquois League of Five Nations formed (later League of Six Nations)
1492	Christopher Columbus arrives on the island of San Salvador in the West Indies
1513	Ponce de Léon and Spanish explorers arrive in Florida
1572	End of Spanish Conquest in North America
1620	Pilgrims arrive at Plymouth Harbor, Massachusetts
1636–1637	Pequot War in Connecticut against the Narrangansett Indians and the English colonists
1643–1701	The Iroquois Wars against French-allied troops in the Northeast
1754–1763	The French and Indian War
1675	King Philip's War of combined tribes against English colonists in Massachusetts
1680	Pueblo tribes join together and drive out Spaniards
1682	The Great Treaty with Lenni Lenape in Shackamaxon, Pennsylvania
1700	Hopi Traditionalists massacre Hopi Awatovi pueblo
1737	Walking Purchase Treaty in Pennsylvania
1776	American Revolution
1783	Iroquois League of Six Nations disbanded
1805	Lewis and Clark Expedition arrives in the Plateau
1817–1858	Seminole Wars
1830–1838	Trail of Tears
1834	End of Mission Period
1835	Surrender of Geronimo
1846–1868	Apache Wars
1848	Gold prospectors flow into California
1856–1858	Yakima Wars in the Plateau and Pacific Coast
1861–1865	Civil War in United States
1863	The Long Walk to Bosque Redondo, New Mexico
1872	Yellowstone National Park established

1872–1874 Period of greatest buffalo slaughter

1874 Battle of Little Bighorn (Custer's Last Stand)

1877 Chief Joseph's Retreat

1882 President Arthur establishes Hopi Reservation in Arizona

1887 Dawes Allotment Act (Indian Allotment Act)

1890 Wounded Knee Massacre

1924 All Native Americans granted citizenship

1934 Indian Reorganization Act (also known as Wheeler-Howard Act)

1944 National Congress of American Indians formed

1953 Beginning of Indian Termination Policy

1970 President Nixon ends termination policy

1991 Creation of Inter-Tribal Bison Cooperative

BOOKS:

Ashburn, P.M. *TheRanks of Death: A Medical History of the Conquest of America.* New York: Coward McCann, 1947.

Collier, John. *The Indians of the Americas.* New York: W.W. Norton, 1947.

Farb, Peter. *Man's Rise to Civilization as Shown by the Indians of North America From Primeval Times to the Coming of the Industrial State.* New York: E.P. Dutton & Co, 1968, 2nd ed, 1978.

Griffin-Pierce, Trudy. *Encyclopedia of Native America.* New York: Viking, 1995.

Gross, Sandra, and Roberts, Jeffrey P. William Penn: Visionary & Proprietor (An Exhibit Catalog). Philadelphia: Atwater Kent Museum.

Hoyt Edwin P. *America's Wars and Military Excursions.* New York: McGraw-Hill, 1987.

Jacobs, Wilbur R. *Dispossessing the American Indian.* New York: Charles Scriber's Sons, 1972.

Kelley, Alison T. Buffalo Bill. *Cobblestone: The Magazine that Makes American History Come Alive.* 1991.

Kraft, Herbert C. *The Lenape or Delaware Indians.* South Orange, NJ: Seton Hall University Museum, 1996.

Lepthien, Emily U. *Buffalo.* Chicago: Children's Press, 1989.

Maas, Peter. The Broken Promise. *Parade Magazine,* September 9, 2001.

Maills, Thomas E. *The Hopi Survival Kit.* New York: Penguin Books, 1997.

Maxwell, James, ed. *America's Fascinating Indian Heritage.* Pleasantville, NY: The Readers Digest Association, 1978.

McCutcheon, David (translated and annotated). *The Red Reord: The Wallum Olum. The Oldest Native North American History.* Garden City Park, NY: Avery Publishing Group, 1993.

Rivinus, Willis M. *William Penn and the Lenape Indians.* New Hope, PA: Willis M. Rivinus, 1995.

Soderlund, Jean R. *William Penn and the Founding of Pennsylvania (1680–1684).* Philadelphia: University of Pennsylvania Press, 1983.

Swanson, Diane. *Buffalo Sunrise. The Story of a North American Giant.* San Francisco: Sierra Club Books, 1996.

Thomas, David Hurst. *Skull Wars.* New York: Basic Books, 2000.

Viola, Herman J, and Margolis, Carolyn. *Seeds of Change.* Washington and London: Smithsonian Institution Press, 1991.

Wallace, Paul AW. *Indians in Pennsylvania,* 2nd ed. Harrisburg, PA: The Pennsylvania Historical and Museum Commission, 1991.

Wilker, Josh. *The Lenape Indians.* Chelsea House Publishers, 1994.

WEB SITES:

http://www.census.gov/
www.scenic-idaho.com/ChiefJosephFoundation/
www.indiantrust.com (lawsuit by Blackfeettribe)
http://www.wnet.org/nature/buffalo/herd/html
http://www.wnet.org/nature/buffalo/strength.html
www.scenic-idaho.com/missioncreekappaloosas/us.htm

PICTURE CREDITS

page:
6: Courtesy of the Library of Congress
11: Associated Press, AP
14: Smithsonian National Museum of the American Indian
19: Courtesy of the Library of Congress
23: Courtesy of the Library of Congress
26: Hulton Archive by Getty Images
30: Smithsonian National Museum of the American Indian
35: Courtesy of the Library of Congress
37: Map by Gary Tong
40: Smithsonian National Museum of the American Indian
44: © Christie's Images/Corbis
47: Map by Gary Tong
49: Courtesy of the Library of Congress
51: Courtesy of the Library of Congress
54: Courtesy of the Library of Congress
56: Courtesy of the Library of Congress
59: Map by Gary Tong
62: © Baldwin H. Ward and Kathryn C. Ward/Corbis
65: Courtesy of the Library of Congress
69: Smithsonian Institution National Anthropological Archives
73: Courtesy of the Library of Congress
75: Courtesy of the Library of Congress
77: Hulton Archive by Getty Images
79: Courtesy of the Library of Congress
85: Courtesy of the Library of Congress
88: Smithsonian Institution National Anthropological Archives
92: Hulton Archive by Getty Images
95: Smithsonian National Museum of the American Indian
97: Smithsonian National Museum of the American Indian
101: Courtesy of the Library of Congress
110: Associated Press, AP
112: Associated Press, AP

ALISON TURNBULL KELLEY holds a BA in Classical Languages from Chestnut Hill College. She is working toward her PhD in holistic nutrition. A freelance writer and editor of medical textbooks and articles for many years, she has also published articles and a play for young people. She lives in Newtown, Bucks County, Pennsylvania.